Making Links

A Collaborative Approach
to Planning and Practice
in Early Childhood Programs

JANET GONZALEZ-MENA
ANNE STONEHOUSE

TEACHERS
COLLEGE
PRESS

Teachers College, Columbia University
New York and London

Published by Teachers College Press, 1234 Amsterdam Avenue, New York, NY
10027

This work was originally published in 2004 by Pademelon Press, 7/3 Packard
Avenue, Castle Hill, New South Wales, 2154, Australia

Library of Congress Cataloging-in-Publication Data

Gonzalez-Mena, Janet.
    Making links : a collaborative approach to planning and practice in early
    childhood programs / Janet Gonzalez-Mena, Anne Stonehouse.
        p. cm.
    Includes bibliographical references and index.
    ISBN 978-0-8077-4843-5 (pbk. : alk. paper)
        1. Child care services. 2. Child care. 3. Child care workers. 4. Family.
    5. Education, Preschool. I. Stonehouse, Anne. II. Title.
    HQ778.5.G66 2008
    362.71′20684—dc22   2007028596

ISBN 978-0-8077-4843-5 (paper)

Printed on acid-free paper
Manufactured in the United States of America

15 14 13 12 11 10 09 08   8 7 6 5 4 3 2 1

Contents

Preface to the Teachers College
    Press Edition   v

Introduction   ix

1. A Perspective on
    Curriculum   1

What This Book Is About   2

Authentic Experiences   4

A Broad Approach to Planning   7

Parents and Children as
Partners with Practitioners   12

A Positive Image of the Child   12

Discipline and Guidance   13

Diversity and Inclusion   14

Looking Forward   14

2. The Adults in
    Children's Experiences:
    Parents and Professionals
    in Collaboration   15

Diversity   16

The Nature of Parent–
Professional Collaboration   19

Partnerships Are Different
from Parent Involvement   21

Communication Is Central   22

The Nature of Communication   28

Communication Strategies   31

Conclusion   33

Looking Forward   33

3. Sources of Knowledge,
    Foundations for Practice   34

Professional Knowledge   34

The Child in the
Context of the Family   40

Aims and Philosophy   43

Colleagues   44

The Community   45

Current Events   47

Geographical and
Environmental Context   48

Yourself   48

Conclusion   49

Looking Forward   49

4. What's Worth Knowing About Each Child   **50**

Introduction to Our ABCs of Knowledge   51

Attachment   53

Body   56

Culture   60

Development   64

Empowerment   67

Fears   70

Group Behavior   74

Home   78

Interactions   83

Judgment   89

Knowledge   93

Learning Styles   96

Major Life Events   98

Needs   101

Outstanding Qualities   105

Play   107

Questions   111

Relationships   113

Special Issues   116

Temperament   121

Understandings   125

Voice   129

Will   132

Xploration   136

Yearnings   138

Zones of Proximal Development   141

Looking Forward   144

5. Gathering Information and Planning   **145**

Information About Every Child and More   147

Ways of Gathering Information   153

Principles of Planning   159

Planning Systems and Formats   162

Looking Forward   164

6. Action Based on Collaboration   **165**

In the End, It's About Culture   165

Collaboration   171

Postscript   174

References   **175**

Index   **177**

About the Authors   **182**

Preface to the Teachers College Press Edition

EARLY CARE AND EDUCATION AS A PROFESSION is growing up, and at the moment it is going through some growing pains. We who are in the profession used to operate without much attention from others, but now policy makers and other people in power are waking up to the fact that, as the slogan goes, "The first years last forever." The field of ECE is the focus of much attention these days in the United States. That attention is pushing us to define our values, to explain ourselves, and to stand strong on our ethics.

In the United States, three historic events began to bring early care and education into the public eye. The first was the federal government's development of child care centers during World War II. The second was Head Start, which grew out of the civil rights movement and President Johnson's war on poverty in the 1960s. The third was the "Ready-to-Learn" campaign of the state governors in the 1990s, which was designed to get children geared up for school before they reached 5 years of age.

Since the end of the last century individuals and agencies who are not versed in child development and early learning have been putting pressure on early childhood professionals. Outsiders have their own ideas about what young children should be doing in our programs. You could say that there is a strong push for the "schoolification" of early childhood.

Some ECE professionals have resisted the forces that called for practices they are philosophically uncomfortable with, such as some of the testing procedures designed to make programs accountable. But as Betsy Hiteshew, a long-time leader in ECE, once said, "The train is leaving the station whether we are on it or not. If we don't get on board, our profession will be determined by outsiders."

So we're on board and working hard to define quality by creating standards, curriculum frameworks, desired results, assessment procedures, and program guides. We're on board a train powered by those who demand accountability and standardization. As we move swiftly forward, will we lose sight of the most important aspects of early care and education? Will the goals still be for children to develop to their full potential, to be who they are, to enjoy their early years? Will professionals still see young children as competent, capable, and creative human beings deserving of full respect? Will the ECE profession retain its integrity?

This book, written to be thought provoking, is designed to help readers slow down that train we're on and take a close look at what is happening in the field. Many of the trends are due to the growing focus on school readiness and universal preschool for 4-year-olds. Some of these trends are:

- the acceleration of childhood
- a focus on objectives and outcomes, instead of on children's experiences
- a disregard of center-based child care and home-based family child care as educational programs

We contend that, just because one program is labeled "educational" and the other focuses on child care, there's no reason that they can't both be educational. Every minute of a child's day can contain both quality care and effective education, if professionals broaden their view of what it takes to support learning and development and of what constitutes important learning in the early years.

This book helps readers see the importance of planning for all the time that children are in a program, not just particular times labeled as "educational." That doesn't mean all-day school; it means moving from an emphasis on narrowly conceived outcomes and the activities to reach them. It means moving toward examining how to make provisions for children to have increasing numbers of authentic experiences—the kinds of experiences that children choose for themselves when presented with choices in an appropriate environment. Of course, the adult's role is to support those choices and offer any resources they might need to take their learning further. What we propose is a huge contrast to learning activities that are fashioned to help children pass tests or move up the developmental scale.

But what about school readiness? We know that offering a range of authentic experiences that take into account family, culture, community, and context, and that are interesting to children in the present, is the best way to prepare them for school and for life.

Our approach is designed to honor diversity, to keep children connected to their families, and to create an equitable relationship between family members and the professionals who serve them.

We hope that you will find the book challenging, thought provoking, and, at the same time, affirming.

A NOTE ABOUT TERMINOLOGY

The information in this book applies equally to both our countries; however, the terminology may cause some confusion, because the vocabulary used about early childhood care and education isn't always the same in the United States and in Australia. We've tried to use terms in this edition of the book that are likely to be familiar to readers in the United States, but that was difficult.

For example, the terms *ECE services* and *children's services* are used in Australia. A simple translation to American English is *early care and education programs*. We are focusing on the programs that serve young children from birth to 5 years and their families that are designated as child care or preschool, whether half-day or full-day, whether home- or center-based. We appreciate your patience if you come across other terms that don't quite fit for you.

Janet Gonzalez-Mena
Anne Stonehouse
August 2007

Introduction

THIS BOOK IS A COLLABORATION BETWEEN two early childhood professionals who enjoy writing and who share a vision of the kind of early childhood program that we would aim for if we were running one, or that we would be happy to have our children (or grandchildren!) attend. We wrote the book because we wanted to work together on a substantial writing project. We have written journal articles together on several occasions, enjoyed the process, and were pleased with the product that resulted from bringing together the two perspectives.

We both have long-standing involvement in early care and education and a special interest in infant and toddler care, parent–professional partnerships, diversity, and family child care.

Our aim is to articulate our vision and ways that it can be achieved. The reason we wanted to do this is not because we think our vision is "right" or "best," but because we believe that by writing our ideas down for others to read, discuss, debate, and think about, we will encourage practitioners to look at their vision and think about their practice. We hope and expect that readers will find the book both affirming and challenging. Our hope is that it will be used collaboratively, and in it we have asked many questions and made a number of suggestions to encourage debate and dialogue.

We have written the book for people working in the early childhood field, in full-day child care and drop-in child care centers, family child care, preschools, kindergartens, mobile programs, and play groups, as well as for students preparing to work in those kinds of programs. The book is relevant for both formally qualified practitioners and for people who do not have formal qualifications.

The focus of the book is children from birth to 5 years old. Our firm belief is that most of the key principles that inform practice with babies and toddlers also inform practice with 3- to 5-year-olds. We also believe that, in spite of differences in names of service types, histories, funding and regulating arrangements, traditions, and community and professional perceptions, all successful early care and education programs share many important characteristics. These common characteristics are the focus of this book.

The book began with a request from the Australian publisher (in 1996!) for one of us to develop some checklists to support the fairly new Quality Improvement and Accreditation System (QIAS) for full-day child care centers in Australia. More specifically, there was within the QIAS a requirement that centers keep developmental records of children and also that they document their planning in written form. This led to requests for forms and checklists.

Needless to say, in the substantial amount of time since that request, there has been considerable evolution in the concept for the book. Having resisted the idea of simply producing forms and checklists, we arrived at the idea of writing a book that focused on what you need to know about children and their families, how you translate that information into plans and practice in programs, and ways to engage parents in the process and to collaborate with them. In fact, two possible titles for the book for some time were *Knowing Children and Using That Knowledge* and *Working Together to Work It Out*. The book has continued to evolve until its publication.

The book is divided into six chapters. They are:

1. A Perspective on Curriculum
2. The Adults in Children's Experiences:
   Parents and Professionals in Collaboration
3. Sources of Knowledge, Foundations for Practice
4. What's Worth Knowing About Each Child
5. Gathering Information and Planning
6. Action Based on Collaboration

We acknowledge that there are many other excellent resource materials available to practitioners, and we assume that these will be used along with this book. Therefore, we have made no attempt to duplicate the wealth of information that practitioners can find elsewhere. Another expectation is that this book will be read and used as a whole. Chapters have a different focus, but are closely interrelated and sequenced intentionally, meaning that the content will be much more meaningful when each chapter is used in the context of the whole book.

The style is informal on purpose. We wanted to convey a sense of having a discussion with the reader, inviting the reader to bring her or his wisdom and experience to the discussion. We see the book as a collaborative encounter with readers.

Janet Gonzalez-Mena
Anne Stonehouse

A Perspective on Curriculum

W ENDY, A TEAM LEADER IN A CHILD CARE CENTER, and Helen, a family child care provider, are chatting one day over coffee. "We just started using a new curriculum at our center for the 3- to 5-year-olds," Wendy announces to her friend, looking pleased.

"Oh, what does it look like?" asks Helen. Then she adds with a quizzical look on her face, "What do you mean when you say curriculum, anyway?"

"Oh, you know, a collection of themes and activities. There's this kit and it comes with a whole year's worth. Everything is there—activities, goals and outcomes, lesson plans, checklists. It even includes posters and some of the materials you need for the activities. They have books that go with each theme. It's organized by seasons and holidays—very complete!"

Helen looks doubtful. "Well, if that's a curriculum, then I already have one." She perks up, "I just call it my program. But I guess I could call it my curriculum—I should sell it!"

"What do you mean?" Wendy looks curious. "I didn't think family child care providers were supposed to have a curriculum."

"Well, I never called it that, but I have group times all organized around themes and then I do follow-up table activities to reinforce them and give the children hands-on experiences with the concepts. I've been doing it for years. It makes it easy and keeps parents happy that their children are having structured learning times. I write it all up ahead of time on these forms that I borrowed from the local preschool, and I put those up for the parents to read. But, to tell you the truth, I'm not entirely happy with it."

"It doesn't work or what?" says Wendy.

"Well, you know, it works; but what I like best is the rest of the day after we get all that over with. I like hanging around with the children while they play, or getting them to help me with some of the work in the garden, or walking to the shops with them to buy our snack. That stuff isn't really part of what I plan for, but there are lots of, what do you call them, 'teachable moments,' and I get to know the children really well. And it just seems more interesting and fun for them and for me."

"Hmmm," said Wendy, and then she changes the subject.

Wendy and Helen seem to think that a curriculum is a collection of activities organized around themes, but we have a different idea. In this book we will be talking about a different kind of curriculum, but we use that word only occasionally and very carefully. We have found that some people avoid it and think it is pretentious and inappropriate, while those who do use it have different ideas about what it means. Many think of packages or books they have seen. Others connect the word with a course of study in an academic institution and have to stretch to understand curriculum as it applies to early childhood care and education. Still others think of it as meaning structure and regimentation and don't think it's right for ECE programs.

We don't need a long Latin word to describe the adult's role in children's learning, growth, and development. We intend to do just that in plain English words throughout this book. We won't avoid the terms *curriculum* and *program*, which seem to be used to mean similar things, but we use them sparingly, to refer to the range of opportunities provided for children in an early childhood program.

WHAT THIS BOOK IS ABOUT

In comparison with the past, there is now greater recognition that early experiences are important in shaping children's development, attitudes toward others, and attitudes toward learning—in other words, experiences matter. This recognition has led to an emphasis on collecting information about children, sometimes called developmental records. It has also resulted, in some places, in increased attention to systematic programming or planning in both center- and home-based child-care services. Understanding that both models provide important developmental and educational experiences for children means that daily practice is now being conceptualized and explained increasingly in terms of a formal curriculum or curriculum framework. These trends come from both increasing requirements for greater accountability to parents, sponsors, regulating authorities, and funding bodies, and from various accreditation and quality assurance systems. Although the idea of paying more attention to what is happening to children is a good one, sometimes the focus is too much on "what to do." Instead of focusing on so-called educational activities, our focus is on knowing and respecting the individual child and the group as a basis for practice.

The knowledge of the child guides practice. There's no use knowing and understanding the child unless that knowledge plays itself out in the child's daily experience in the program. This is where things become a bit more complicated—translating knowledge *about* children into practices *with* and provisions *for* children. In other words, sometimes, because of time or pressures or methods adopted for planning, the links between what is known about children and their experiences are not as strong as they could be. Many things get in the way of making those links strong. Making those links is what this book is about.

This book is also about creating an environment, experiences, interactions, and relationships that allow children from birth to age 5 to have authentic experiences that will promote their growth, development, and learning. It's about building relationships that are the foundation for the teaching/learning process. It's about getting to know each child in order to tailor that environment, those interactions, experiences, and relationships to fit the individual, while at the same time taking into account the group as a whole. It's about incorporating the families of the children into the decisions and implementation of the teaching and learning process. It's about dealing with all the kinds of diversity that are part of any early childhood program and doing so in ways that enrich everyone's lives and help children live in a world that exposes them increasingly to differences of all kinds. In a nutshell, this book is about knowing children and using the knowledge to plan and provide for children's experiences.

We are talking about a plan of action designed to tap into each child in ways that are in accordance with the family's culture, goals, priorities, and dreams for their child. In a few words, we're talking about *a plan for learning*, which is one definition of the word *curriculum*. Of course, when that plan is put into action, there has to be a lot of thinking, altering the plan, and moving right away from the plan. In addition, unexpected things happen; but the plan, that is, the intentions of the adults, still guides what actually happens. Intentions are always kept in mind.

This book is aimed at all people who work with young children in early childhood programs. We use the word *practitioner* or *professional* to mean an *early childhood educator* who works in any setting geared for the care and education of young children. We don't separate care and education. You cannot focus on the mind of a child without focusing on the body and feelings as well. Our approach to curriculum is a holistic one, as is our approach to children themselves. We see care and education as part of the same package.

We intend this book to be a practical resource without being a "how to" book. It isn't a do-all, be-all book, and should be used alongside other resources. We hope to help readers fit the pieces together, rather like a mosaic. A mosaic is a good metaphor for the book because of the idea of putting pieces together to form a whole. It's a mosaic, not a puzzle, because there are many good ways to put the pieces together. The outcome is original, a work of art and craft.

As you can see from the opening scene, our aim is to include different program types, both family child care and center-based programs. In addition, we are writing this book for people who are working in or preparing to work in sessional programs, occasional care programs, and play groups, as well as enrichment, early intervention, and inclusion programs.

We emphasize diversity throughout the book rather than dealing with it in a particular place. We will include the whole age range of early childhood education; that is, from birth to school entry age (typically 5).

In our book, planning for learning goes way beyond the themes and activities that Helen and Wendy saw as curriculum. We resist laying things out for a year at a time, disregarding who is in the program, what changes occur with the children as the year goes on, what's happening in the children's lives or in the community, or what interests the children. Our idea of curriculum (or a plan for learning) relates specifically to the children in the program, their strengths and interests as individuals and as a group, and what their families want.

There are linking concepts that run through the entire book. They are:

1. authentic experiences;
2. a broad approach to planning;
3. parents and children as partners with practitioners;
4. a positive image of the child;
5. discipline and guidance; and
6. diversity and inclusion.

The first two concepts relate to reflection, planning, and what constitutes the curriculum.

AUTHENTIC EXPERIENCES

There's more to early childhood care and education than just planning activities around themes, or even not around themes, as Wendy and Helen suggested. Our vision of what should happen in practice is that adults think beyond activities and create many opportunities for children to have a variety of authentic experiences, many of which take place naturally in the context of the day or session. When the adults' energy goes into creating activities, the result may not be as meaningful.

Here's a scene we've both seen various versions of. Wendy is "doing snow" because her curriculum is based on seasons. It happens to be a sunny winter day and it is fairly warm outside, but she has been told that all children should know about snow, even if it never snows where they live. She read a story about snow during group time, but the children were restless and she had to hurry through it. Now she has two activities set up so children have a choice. At one table they are tracing and cutting lots of white paper circles of three sizes, and they have dark blue paper to paste them on. Wendy's idea is that they will make snow people. At another table Wendy is showing children how to fold paper and cut snowflakes. Before anyone has accomplished anything, three children are at the door complaining that they'd rather be outside. One child at the snowflake table is crying because she can't do it properly, and she keeps cutting the paper into pieces and then needing to start over. There's a pile of paper on the floor by her chair. When Wendy discovers that a left-handed child is trying to use right-handed scissors, she scurries around trying to discover what happened to the left-handed ones. In the meantime, at the other table, one child is cutting more than his share of circles and gluing them all over the paper, some on the table as well. Another child is crumpling the paper and making balls and throwing them. "Oh," Wendy remarks to him in a friendly voice, "You know about snowballs." "No," he says, "These are baseballs." The girl he has been throwing them at cries. What do you think the children learned about snow from those activities?! Are some of these experiences meaningful ones? Which ones? Are they desirable experiences even if meaningful?

Let's look in on Helen's family child care home. She too is doing an activity. The theme is softness. She has gathered a variety of materials for collage and has them arranged neatly on the kitchen table. Most of the children are seated on chairs, but the one 2-year-old prefers to stand. Wendy is holding the 8-month-old to keep her out of the way, but the baby is desperate to get her hands on the collage materials. The 2-year-old has pulled the container of glue over by him and squeezed it onto an empty paper plate. He then helps himself to a cotton ball and is scrubbing the bottom of the paper plate vigorously, saturating the cotton ball. Helen hands him a piece of paper and suggests he stick it on there, but he chooses to stick it in his hair instead before she can stop him. While she is at the sink cleaning him up, the rest of the children, inspired by their friend's creativity, start sticking cotton balls all over themselves and then on each other. Helen gives up on the activity and gets them to start cleaning up. All the time she's thinking about the floating and sinking activity she has planned for tomorrow. She imagines that it will make a big mess too!

We can imagine both Wendy's and Helen's stress levels in the scenes above. The adult may have had a clear goal in mind, but what the children are actually learning in these situations bears little resemblance to what the adult had in mind! The adult spends time supervising both the children and the materials and little time interacting and communicating in ways that support desirable learning. Our observations of adults doing activities with children lead us to think these are not always the times when the best learning occurs or when relationships are enhanced.

Nothing is wrong with what either Wendy or Helen is trying to do, but the energy and stress on their part is substantial and the results are of questionable value. Other examples we've seen are adults stopping children from rich dramatic play to do a matching game with numbers or letters. Almost any group time with more than three toddlers qualifies as an example of an activity that yields far different results from what adults plan. Our experience shows us that taking an activity approach to enhancing learning and development means that the adults spend a lot of time and energy planning, preparing, directing, and cleaning up the activities. When that happens, the rest of the day becomes a time out from learning while the adult recovers from the mess and strain of the activities. How else is the adult to have strength to get through the rest of the day? The day then becomes segmented into three parts—activity time, free play, and routines. When activities are the focus, there's a tendency not to give much thought to the other parts of the day. Free play is seen as a time for children to relax or let off steam—a time out from learning while the adult gathers energy. The eating, grooming, toileting/diaper changing, and sleeping/resting times may not be looked at as valuable learning times, but rather as tasks to get through as quickly and efficiently as possible. Children's potential for learning is there all the time.

From our perspective, adults should be occupied more with children than with activities and what they may consider chores. This focus on children can happen most effectively when children have authentic experiences and spend their days in environments that are rich, that invite exploration, testing, and figuring things out. In these environments adults can put their energy into interacting with children rather than organizing and supervising educational activities. They can include the children in those essential tasks of everyday living, so that they become wonderful times for learning. Eating, for example, can become a social time. That's different from adults just serving food to children and monitoring their eating. When diaper changing becomes a time of one-to-one interaction with the adult and child both paying attention to each other and the activity, that's different from an adult just concentrating on a bare bottom. When the task alone is the focus, the rest of the child is often ignored unless he's struggling to get off the changing table.

A major adult role is planning for and enhancing children's learning and development. We envision curriculum as the result of planning that focuses on the children themselves. We propose that, rather than putting together a long succession of planned learning activities, energy is better spent thinking about the many varied experiences the children have when adults continually create *opportunities for learning* and support children to create them too. Such an approach is different from an activity-oriented curriculum in that it happens all day long when adults organize the environment and make materials available in it. They take note of how the environment affects the experiences and interactions and make adjustments when necessary. Some of these experiences include the interactions that happen during essential activities of daily living—caregiving routines such as feeding and eating times, toileting, napping, and grooming.

Other experiences grow out of more general interactions involving communication between children and adults and among the children themselves. Every experience holds potential for learning.

In summary, our notion of curriculum, which we think of as a *plan for learning,* is holistic and comprehensive in that it encompasses everything, not just specific kinds of structured activities, such as group time. When Helen talked about the parts of her child care day that interested her most, she wasn't talking about the structured activities that she considered learning times, but rather the ones in which she and the children had more authentic interactions, those parts of the day she considered outside the curriculum. We include those other times and in fact highlight them as effective learning times. The interactions and activities that interest both the adult and children the most are the ones that help children make important connections—connections with people, with things, and with ideas. When children are making connections, they become involved in the community. The community of the early childhood programs (whether center-based or family child care) becomes a model for children to learn the skills of getting along with one another and prepares them for their role in the larger community.

A BROAD APPROACH TO PLANNING

One of the signs that an early childhood program is professional, that it offers more than just looking after children, is that it offers a *program.* This term usually designates the part of the day or session that is planned ahead of time and carefully thought out, with a focus on educational activities. We think that planning should be broader than that. Maybe you are thinking that our approach is too loose. Emphasizing times other than those of structured, planned activities doesn't mean that we think no planning needs to occur—that children are just on their own "doing their own thing" and we just assume or hope that learning occurs. Quite the contrary. We believe in careful attention to detail. We believe that thinking carefully ahead of time about what will be provided for children is important—after all, that's what this book is about. What we are advocating is the broadening of thinking and planning to include not just activities, but also the physical environment, both indoors and outdoors; equipment and materials; the way time is structured; interactions and relationships not just with children but between children and with children's families; and daily living experiences such as eating, sleeping and resting, toileting, bathing, dressing and undressing, and even arriving and leaving. These elements of the program have a major impact on whether or not the child has a good experience.

Planning involves thinking about what you *want to* happen and what you think *will* happen and how to blend the two. You have to be prepared for what you have planned, as well as for what you haven't planned.

It seems to us, however, that there is a danger of latching on to the idea of a program and programming as the way to be seen to be working professionally with children, and in the process developing some notions that actually restrict and constrain thinking about what is offered to children. For us, having a program or engaging in the process of programming doesn't mean:

- being rigid or inflexible, sticking to what was planned no matter what;
- filling in a timetable, as though slotting activities into a predetermined timetable is the only way to do it;
- having a plan for every minute of the day or session;
- being locked into certain categories of activities—typically organized by developmental areas, traditional categories of curriculum, or themes;
- the practitioners having all the ideas, instead of listening to and watching to see what interests the children; and
- insisting that every child does the same thing at the same time.

Planning in the way we are thinking about it in this book is having a purposeful idea of what you might do and being prepared, taking careful notice of how things are going while they are happening, and using that information to plan for the future. Let's react to some of the characteristics above and contrast them with some of the characteristics of a different kind of children's experience and the processes that lead to that.

Early childhood programs can be charactertized by:

- flexibility and spontaneity balanced with a sense of purpose and predictability;
- creative thinking;
- working together with children and families to design and implement children's experiences; and
- giving choices.

Let's look at each of these individually.

Flexibility and Spontaneity Balanced
with a Sense of Purpose and Predictability

Having a plan doesn't mean sticking to it no matter what. A plan is an educated guess ahead of time, and only a guess, and there are many reasons for moving away from the plan. These include children's interests, moods, and energy levels; the weather; and staffing constraints, to name a few. Sometimes, unexpected opportunities arise; for example, the road crew and equipment arrive in the street outside. That might be just the time to change plans if the children are flocking to the window to watch. Just as in our personal lives, it makes sense on many occasions to vary a plan. A plan is something to fall back on, a basis for action as long as it makes sense in the context of what is happening.

Of course, it is necessary to have some idea of how the day or session will flow, and a routine is important to help children feel secure and give them a sense of having some control over their own experience. However, there are ways to plan other than according to time slots. Especially when the planning focuses on more than activities, it makes sense to think beyond time slots. While the planning process should encourage practitioners to look critically at the flow of the day or session to see if it supports the kind of experience they want to provide children, planning takes into account and focuses on dimensions of the program other than time slots; for example, the environment, daily living experiences, interactions and relationships, special opportunities, or provisions for play. Planning in this more expansive way frees practitioners up from thinking that planning is merely a matter of filling up a timetable or schedule. A plan needs to incorporate some flexibility in terms of time, to allow for children's interest being greater or less than anticipated. The ECE programs we prefer do not run like clockwork!

Creative Thinking

Often practitioners plan according to predetermined categories. One common way is to use developmental areas. For example, some planning formats list intellectual, large motor, small motor, and emotional or similar terms, and activities are slotted in that support those areas of development. Another common way of doing it is to list categories of activities, such as arts and crafts, music, problem solving, dramatic play, and manipulative, and slot activities in. While it is useful to use different categories to check that the program results in a balance of kinds of experiences, their use can limit thinking about what might be interesting and appropriate for children.

Alternatively, when there is a real focus on figuring out what interests the children and how that can be nurtured and extended in appropriate ways, then the result is likely to be a richer, more exciting array of offerings.

Working with Children and Families

Practitioners have ultimate responsibility to do the planning, but they do it in collaboration with children and families. We think the best programs for children happen when practitioners get their ideas not only from their own expertise and experience but also from children's interests expressed and observed, parents' ideas, and events and issues in the community. When we use the term *parents* we mean anyone who takes a parenting role, not necessarily the children's birth or biological parents. We interchange *family* with *parent* throughout the book in recognition that most children come from a family context, whether a biological extended family or a kinship network. Sometimes the person responsible for the decisions concerning the child's care and education is not the parent. Practitioners need to recognize the hierarchies involved. Understanding and respecting the elevated status of elders is part of this recognition in many cases.

Giving Choices

There is a view that planning necessarily means group activities, insisting that every child does the same thing at the same time. Not at all—it is just as easy to plan for choices, children's initiative, and variety as it is to plan for the opposite. And there are many advantages in the former: children's interests are catered to, they are empowered in their own learning, their varying attention spans are respected, and the adult is spared the impossible task of picking the one thing that will capture everyone's interest.

Long ago we learned about the problem of the match (McVicker Hunt, 1961). If learning occurs when there is a good match between what is already known and something new, then the challenge is to make a match for every child. The solution is to provide variety and choices and let the child choose his or her own perfect match.

A Caution About Themes. We suggest giving up the security of themes. Having a theme that ties everything together can make practitioners feel secure and satisfied, because it provides a ready-made rationale for everything they provide. Themes also impress parents. However, themes can limit the inclination to build on children's interests and follow up on what they want to do. It is easy for the theme to become dominant in the practitioner's mind and restrict thinking, so that the major reason for providing or doing something becomes whether or not it fits the theme rather than whether or not it is a worthwhile authentic learning experience for children. The challenge themes provide for adults is to think of varied and unusual ways to implement the theme, but these ways often make little sense to children. Children may not see the links that the adults do. Themes may impress adults, but they may fail the test of *is this authentic and does it support children's understanding of themselves, the physical world, and other people?* A theme should never be an excuse not to respond to children's interest.

A theme of sorts may emerge when a number of children develop a strong interest in a particular topic, and that interest lasts for some time. This is more likely to happen when adults support that interest. We would say that the theme we see as being most important for young children is the theme of "life, other people, the world, and me"! There's nothing wrong with a "theme after the fact"; that is, responding to children's interests may result in a kind of theme. For example, toddlers may be fascinated with babies, or several 4-year-olds with the beach or restaurants or camping or dinosaurs, and one thing leads to another. These retrospective themes are often for only some of the children, while the others pursue their own interests from the range of opportunities, equipment, and materials available. That's a very different matter from the adult thinking in advance about a collection of activities on a particular theme, and doing them with all children to the exclusion of most anything else except the ordinary things that are always available.

A Place for Projects. The term *project* reflects our approach more accurately than themes. Although the term is used in early childhood literature in a variety of ways, the way we are thinking about projects is as a collection of related experiences with an agreed-upon purpose. That purpose might change as the project takes place, but there is always a purpose. The term *project* suggests something focused, having a particular aim, such as constructing a camp in the back of the garden, creating a small vegetable garden, or building a village in the block corner.

Projects usually extend over time, lasting longer than a single activity. Another word sometimes used to describe what we are calling "project" is *investigation*. A project doesn't necessarily have a narrow focus or isn't something that is completed once and for all. A project can be huge and open—like finding out all you can about ships, puppies, or the sky. The secret to successful projects is that they come from children's interests and that the adult really pays attention to what children are wondering about, wanting to do, finding challenging, and where they are wanting to go next. The adult builds on those in ways that are meaningful to children.

Sometimes the children's interest comes from adult interest in something. If the practitioner, family, or community is interested in something, the children become interested too. Passions, whether they reside in a child or in an adult, have a way of becoming contagious. The thing about a worthwhile project is that there is always a kind of authenticity about it—it isn't contrived or something trivial or silly. Projects usually involve small groups of children who show interest. It is possible that a project could take over the entire group of children for a time, if it is of great interest to most of them. However, there is a big difference between allowing that to happen and insisting that it happen by giving no alternatives.

The two linking concepts above, authentic experiences and a broad approach to planning, focus directly on our ideas about what constitutes the curriculum. Four more linking concepts follow. One of these, "Parents and children as partners with practitioners" is found in every chapter, but has a chapter of its own as well. The other three principles are woven throughout the book.

PARENTS AND CHILDREN
AS PARTNERS WITH PRACTITIONERS

Working together with children and families to design and implement children's experience is a major thread in this book. Children may be the recipients of care and education, but planning for learning involves a three-way collaboration. Children can contribute as well as their parents. Parents and families are not just the people the children go home to after the end of the day or session; they are the mainstay of the children's lives. They are the ones with dreams, visions, goals, and values concerning their children's future. As such they must be regarded as not only recipients of the service, but also major players. They need to be in on the decisions that concern their children. We aren't talking about parent involvement on a superficial level, such as worker bees cleaning up the outside areas or taking smocks home to wash. Certainly that kind of involvement is worthwhile, but we are talking about partnerships. You'll see that communication with parents is a major feature of this book. It has already come up in the section above and you'll find it throughout.

A POSITIVE IMAGE OF THE CHILD

Our approach comes from a perspective that sees children as capable and resourceful, rather than as weak, underdeveloped, and needy (NSW Department of Community Services, 2002). Not all approaches take this perspective. For example, one approach to children's learning follows a medical model; that is, adults diagnose and prescribe. They ask themselves questions such as "What does this child lack? What are the gaps, the weaknesses, the needs?" Diagnostic tools are used to determine the problems and then prescriptions are applied. For example, one child is diagnosed with, among other things, poor listening skills. The prescription is to sit her down, get her to do listening activities, and stop her from running around outside, which she loves to do and where she shows advanced physical abilities, strength, and coordination. Another child loves cutting with scissors and drawing intricate pictures, but hates climbing on the outdoor equipment and anything related to running and jumping. The prescription is to restrict his time indoors and take him outside to work with him until he develops good physical coordination.

With this approach the focus is on the things children can't do rather on what they can do. Children are assessed and compared to each other. Even the ones who, by comparison, are ahead of the rest have some gaps and weaknesses, so they get the message that they aren't there yet, wherever "there" is. Some children grow up with a much stronger sense of their deficits or weaknesses than they do of their assets. We propose that focusing on strengths instead of weaknesses is more useful because children gain self-confidence when they are encouraged to do what they are good at doing. That self-confidence helps them expand their horizons. They use their strengths to further their knowledge and understanding of the world around them while gaining skills to interact effectively with it. As their world and skills expand they see reasons to add to what they already know and can do. An inner urge (intrinsic motivation) moves them to increase particular skills and knowledge they need to pursue their interests and capitalize on their strengths. This inner urge replaces the need for a good deal of outside motivation in the form of rewards from adults or competition with other children.

Of course adults also must keep an eye on the areas where children need encouragement and help. Although we focus on strengths, adults still need to encourage and support children to try things they aren't good at. Also, part of the early childhood practitioner's job is to take a role in identifying children with special needs and challenges, including developmental delays.

DISCIPLINE AND GUIDANCE

Just because we see children as capable doesn't mean that they don't have a lot to learn. One big area of learning is expanding children's knowledge about acceptable behavior. Helping children learn what to do and what not to do, what is desirable and undesirable, is commonly referred to as discipline or guidance. Discipline and guidance are important subjects, but instead of making them a separate chapter, we have embedded them throughout. This book is about learning, and some of the most important things to learn in the first 5 years are how to look after yourself, get along with others, and take care of the physical environment. That, in fact, is our definition of what is usually called discipline, guidance, or behavior management. Some people think of these under the label of "learning to behave," which reflects the fact that many people think of discipline as getting children to do the right thing and to not do the wrong thing, or "teaching them to behave."

Often in discussions of working with children, and in books and other resources, discipline is separated out as a topic, as though it is unrelated to the other kinds of teaching and learning that go on in an early childhood program. We have a different view. We see that the ways of learning to look after yourself, others, and the world around you are no different from learning other kinds of things about how the world works, how to do things, and how to relate to others. That means that the principles involved in all learning apply to learning to behave in desirable ways and learning to control your own behavior. And that, after all, is the aim of what is often referred to as discipline.

DIVERSITY AND INCLUSION

Instead of creating separate chapters on diversity, inclusion, and special needs, we have chosen to integrate them throughout the book. We hope you will observe where these topics occur and take special notice of them. If you don't already have them integrated in your mind when you start this book, we hope that by the end you will remember to include them every time you think about or discuss early care and education.

LOOKING FORWARD

So now read on, keeping the pieces of a mosaic in mind. The first mosaic pieces we want to present are the adults in children's experiences. We see collaboration between parents and practitioners, so we will focus on both those groups of adults in the next chapter, exploring how partnerships translate into daily practice that results in better outcomes for children.

2

The Adults in Children's Experiences: Parents and Professionals in Collaboration

THE LINK BETWEEN PARENTS AND PRACTITIONERS is central to this book. The importance of working closely with parents and family on behalf of the child cannot be overestimated. A number of different terms can be used to describe the relationship that is desirable. The two that we like best are *collaboration* and *partnerships*. Both terms suggest working closely together to achieve a common goal. In the case of ECE programs, that common goal is children's well-being and learning.

Although this book assumes a view of children as powerful contributors to their own experience, and therefore to their development and learning, adults are the main agents, the gatekeepers, for children's experience. Adults make the decisions about what the child has access to, what materials and equipment are available, and, most important, what interactions and relationships are possible. We know that the quality and nature of their relationships and interactions have a profound effect on children's pictures of themselves as well as on their learning. Children are never passive recipients of what the practitioner provides. In our view, children inevitably impact the design and implementation of the curriculum, whether or not adults acknowledge this. Ideally, adults do acknowledge and capitalize on the contribution children make, and support and enhance their power to affect their experience. However, inevitably and justifiably, adults have more power than children.

One of the fundamental premises of this book is that outcomes are better for everyone when parents and practitioners work in partnership on behalf of children and share power. This chapter will explore the concepts of partnership and collaboration, how they translate into daily practice, and the nature of the contributions of parents and practitioners to them.

Our vision of center- and home-based ECE programs at their best is that they are actually family support services. The term *family support service* may make you think that we are talking about a whole complex of integrated services incorporating health, welfare, counseling, medical, early childhood, and other kinds of services all together. There is a wide range of additional services that some ECE programs offer to families. We have even heard of child care centers where parents can drop off and pick up their dry cleaning, and ones that sell meals for parents to take home for the family at the end of the day. There are many advantages when a number of services needed by families are close together, and even greater advantages when they are integrated rather than operating separately. What we want to focus on is not additional services that can be provided, but rather the nature of the relationship that exists between early childhood practitioners and families when the program operates as a family support service. The focus remains on the child, but on the child in the context of her or his family, culture, and community. Having that focus means working closely with the child's family. A program that operates as a family support service operates with clarity that in no way does the service *substitute* for the child's experience in the family, but rather complements it and plays a role in ensuring that the experience in the family is a healthy and constructive one.

When practitioners and parents work in collaboration or partnership, parents and families benefit from their participation by having their relationship with the child supported and their knowledge and appreciation of the child increased. Obviously, then, the child benefits as well. When parents contribute actively to their child's experience in the program, their notions of their own importance in their child's life are strengthened. Active contribution doesn't necessarily mean doing work for the program or even being there, but rather is about discussing, sharing information and concerns, and engaging in shared decision making with practitioners. Working in partnership or collaboration is about sustaining the notion that "we're in this together." Obviously parents play a much more vital role than just being passive recipients of information, advice, and an early childhood experience for their child.

Unfortunately, in the past, practitioners' appreciation of the importance of working with parents has sometimes translated into a license to give parents advice, to tell them how to rear their child. This can have the effect of disempowering parents, making them feel inept, and diminishing their confidence in their ability to rear their child to the child's best benefit.

DIVERSITY

We have said that rather than treating diversity as a separate topic we have integrated it throughout the book, because we believe that issues about diversity affect just about everything you do in an early childhood program. However, there are a few points about diversity that are especially relevant when we are thinking about the relationships that exist between families using the program and the practitioners who work in it.

When we talk about diversity we are not just talking about cultural diversity. There are many kinds of diversity; for example, cultural, racial, linguistic, economic, and lifestyle. People differ in their values, backgrounds, and political views, not to mention the many kinds of diversity that come from what we might label individual differences and uniqueness. Sometimes kinds of diversity other than cultural are harder to come to terms with; that is, when people who look and seem to be like us demonstrate a difference that makes us uncomfortable. It may be easier for people to accept difference when it is thought to be culturally based rather than simply a reflection of lifestyle or personal preference. For example, it may be easier to go along with a child not being allowed to eat pork for religious reasons than to support a family's personal decision to be vegetarians. As another example, maybe it is easier to accept a young child sleeping in the same bed with parents if they are from a different culture from the one you are familiar with than if they just decide to do that because of personal preference. For some people it seems that attributing difference to culture gives it some sort of legitimacy.

In order for a children's program to work effectively, there has to be genuine acceptance and acknowledgment of diversity and a firm belief that the constructive resolution of differences in attitudes, understandings, and perspectives often results in better outcomes, more creativity, and more efficient problem solving. Equally, there has to be an understanding that where people come together for the sake of something important to them—in our case, young children's well-being—there will inevitably be differences in ideas about what is important and how to go about doing things. Sometimes these differences will arouse strong feelings, and conflict is inevitable. This is not necessarily a negative thing, as long as there is the will to resolve differences fairly and constructively and the means to do so. Constructive resolution of conflict results in greater understanding and stronger relationships. In this book we use the term *honoring diversity* rather than *celebrating diversity*, in acknowledgment of the many challenges posed by taking diversity seriously. The kinds of tensions and challenges that come with working in genuine partnership with parents may test the professionalism of practitioners.

One obvious and significant category of diversity that exists in an early childhood program is the perspectives held about children by parents and practitioners. They will inevitably see the child differently. Many parents, because they have such a strong emotional investment in the child, are not able to be objective when it comes to their child.

Typically, and fortunately, the vast majority of parents hold their child in high regard. They may worry about, be puzzled by, and even sometimes be annoyed with their child but, overall, most parents see their child as being very special. That is a good thing, because every child needs someone who thinks they are wonderful!

We must also remind ourselves about the dangers of making generalizations about groups or categories of people and then assuming that those generalizations apply to everyone in that group or category. Embracing diversity means that each parent, each family, is treated as unique, and practitioners resist putting people into categories and generalizing or making assumptions without knowing the facts. In ECE programs we're good at treating each child as an individual, and we need to do that with parents too.

Each parent, each family, and each parent–child relationship is unique. In addition, each practitioner is a unique individual, even though he or she shares professional beliefs and values and a common philosophy with colleagues. Therefore, each relationship between an early childhood professional and a parent is unique.

Having warned about the pitfalls of making generalizations, we are going to make some ourselves! It is safe to say that most parents:

- are very busy;
- have responsibilities and obligations other than rearing the child you work with, and which compete with always doing the absolute best thing with and for the child;
- take time to trust you;
- wonder how they are doing as parents;
- try to be good parents;
- are eager to hear good news about their child;
- dislike hearing not-so-good news about their child;
- want reassurance that their child is developing and learning as expected;
- appreciate indications from you that their child is understood, respected, treated as an individual, and liked; and
- look to you to take the lead in establishing the kind of relationship and communication they will have with you.

Most important, practitioners must recognize that, at a general level, most parents usually want the same things for their child that we do—for the child now and in the future to be healthy, have friends, do well in school and later in work, be clever, make a constructive contribution to society, and be happy and fulfilled. It is easy to lose sight of that fact sometimes when there are differences and tensions between parents and practitioners. Those differences, however, often have to do with how to get there; that is, what are the best ways to ensure that the child has a fulfilling and successful life.

However, although there are things most parents have in common, there is still great diversity among parents:

- some are more open and willing to share information than others;
- some are more confident as people and as parents than others;
- some are more assertive than others;
- some are more critical and demanding than others;
- some have more support than others;
- some have more desire to know details about their child's experience than others, and they have varying degrees of interest in contributing to that experience; and
- some are more interested in and available to get involved than others.

Also, family composition and circumstances are different. Some families live in continual crisis and under great stress. They may be affected by homelessness, violence, chronic illness, drug abuse, poverty, or other circumstances that interfere with them putting the child first, which may mean that meeting the responsibilities of being a "good" parent in the eyes of others who make such judgments is impossible for them. Some parents may appear at times to be irresponsible or even uncaring, and this may be due to the realities of their lives, where there are so many complex issues to deal with that compete with their child rearing.

Practitioners also have to be clear about the boundaries of their professional expertise. In other words, sometimes parents and families may have needs and issues that go beyond what the early childhood program can deal with. Hopefully, at these times, the program can call on other professionals and programs with whom they have partnerships in order to assist the family. ECE programs vary in the resources they can offer, in addition to providing a good early childhood experience for children. When families have needs that extend beyond what the program offers, it is the responsibility of the children's program to help them access the support that they need.

THE NATURE OF PARENT–PROFESSIONAL COLLABORATION

Why is partnership or collaboration with parents important? The reason most people work in ECE programs is because they want to have a long-lasting positive impact on the child. The best way to do this—in fact, some would say the only way to do it—is to work in collaboration or partnership with parents. After all, early childhood practitioners are part of the life of the child and the family for a relatively short period of time in the child's life. Parents and family are with the child for life. And besides, you cannot know what is in the child's best interests without being open to perspectives other than your own. Be careful about thinking you know what is best for a child under any circumstances. When you take into consideration the cultural, family, and community context of the child's life, the complexity of deciding what's best becomes much more evident.

Early childhood practitioners can impact in a major way parents' understanding of their child and the parent–child relationship. The insights and perspectives of practitioners can shape the picture parents hold of their child. We write about empowerment in relation to children and to families in a later chapter. It is critical that ECE programs empower families in terms of their confidence and their appreciation of the impact they have on their child's life. Obviously, when the attitude of the practitioner is "leave it to us, we are the experts," families are disempowered.

So, what is meant by partnership? Just as in a business or personal partnership, the characteristics of a partnership with parents include:

- mutual respect;
- trust;
- sensitivity to the other's perspective and role;
- ongoing, open communication (as opposed to practitioners just reporting or giving advice and requiring certain kinds of "reporting" from parents);
- an absence of rivalry or competition;
- recognition and valuing of the unique contribution and strengths of the partner;
- a good fit between the different strengths of partners (in other words, it's not necessarily a good partnership if both partners are good at the same things); and
- shared decision making.

In ECE programs, there is a tendency to package and compartmentalize things. Thinking this way won't work when it comes to family–professional partnerships. Working collaboratively with families is a culture or way of working that runs through every part of the operation of the program. It isn't something that can be treated as a discrete component. "Partnership is a relationship, a matter of heart and mind, a perspective, not a set of activities or strategies" (Centre for Community Child Health, 2001a, p. 2). It is more than a collection of policies and procedures, or a list of principles in a quality assurance system. All of these things can help to support and strengthen a culture of partnership that is already present, but by themselves they don't bring about genuine partnership. It's also important to remind ourselves that the focus of the partnership is the child's well-being, development, and learning, not the operation of the program, and that leads us to think about the difference between partnership and involvement.

PARTNERSHIPS ARE DIFFERENT FROM PARENT INVOLVEMENT

One obstacle to working in partnership is confusion about what it actually means. Sometimes ECE practitioners use the term *partnership* when they are really talking about *parent involvement*. That's what most early childhood professionals who have been working in the field for some time are familiar with. Traditionally, parent involvement in ECE programs has consisted of parents helping out. Some examples include such things as:

- worker bees and maintenance;
- contribution of materials;
- parent helpers with the children; for example, preparing morning or afternoon snack or coming along on excursions;
- demonstrating to or teaching children because of a special talent or interest; and
- fund raising.

A few other common kinds of parent involvement are:

- organizing and participating in social functions sponsored by the program;
- attending talks and meetings organized by the early childhood program; and
- being a member of the management or parent advisory committee for the program.

Having a variety of ways for parents to be involved in the operation of the program is important, because some parents will want to take up that option. However, it should be just that—an option—rather than a requirement. Doing jobs such as fund raising, serving on the management committee, and helping out in other ways are useful to the program and help parents connect with professionals, feel comfortable, and make contact with other parents, all of which are valuable. It may lead the way to partnership. However, working in partnership with parents is not the same thing as involving parents. Parent involvement opportunities should be seen as a means to an end, not an end in themselves, as a way of forming connections on behalf of the child. The main difference between parent involvement and working in partnership is one that has to do with power. Most traditional kinds of parent involvement leave the power and authority in the hands of the practitioners, unthreatened and uncompromised. That is, the practitioner decides how parents can be involved, and these ways are typically ones that don't threaten the practitioner's authority.

COMMUNICATION IS CENTRAL

Collaboration rests solidly on a foundation of informal, natural, ongoing communication. Sometimes that communication is essential to the child's well-being. In other words, there are times when practitioners and parents *must* share information about things such as signs of illness, changes in the child's schedule, and changes in the arrangements for the child's participation, policies, or matters related to fees.

In addition, there is information that must be shared or the child's experience both at home and in the program will be poorer. These include topics such as:

- changes in circumstances at home or in the program;
- major events in the child's day in the program or, from the parents, important things that happened overnight or on the weekend;
- information about the child's behavior or routine;
- major developmental milestones that have occurred; and
- problems with or concerns about the child's health, behavior, or development.

For there to be genuine collaboration or partnership, communication has to go further than what is essential and minimal.

What happens through an easy natural flow of communication is that both parents and practitioners together build a shared picture of the child (Centre for Community Child Health, 2001b). That is, the parents' perspective when shared alters yours, yours alters the parents', and both continually change as the child changes and as information is shared. Sometimes what is shared is simple and straightforward; for example, when the parent tells you that the child has become fascinated with insects in the garden at home, or you tell the parent that it looks as though their child is showing some interest in using the toilet. If the other hasn't noticed what is being shared, it then becomes part of the picture of the child. Sometimes of course what is shared is like a missing piece of a puzzle. For example, if a parent gives you the startling news that their house was broken into over the weekend, this information helps you "get the picture" of why the child has been clingy and withdrawn. The information may not always be bad news—think of the joy of sharing the excitement when a child has made a beautiful painting, or when a parent reports that his child has mastered the pedals on the tricycle over the weekend.

The result of these interchanges is:

- parents' confidence increases, as does their involvement in their child's life;
- you and the parent operate with greater understanding and appreciation of the child;
- you have the satisfaction of knowing that you are probably making a long-lasting contribution to the child's life; and
- most important, the child has a better experience at home and in the early childhood program.

Parent education is something that is often talked about as important. We prefer not to think of the ongoing communication as "educating parents," although both practitioners and parents will become wiser because of it. Our view is that parents have as much to teach practitioners as practitioners have to teach parents. Early childhood professionals typically have considerable experience of many children and knowledge about children in general. Many of them have wisdom from formal study to share. Parents, on the other hand, know their child, their culture, and their family.

The base or necessary conditions that make parent–practitioner partnerships possible can be categorized into six areas:

1. clarity;
2. confidence;
3. empathy;
4. competence;
5. connections; and
6. commitment.

Clarity

The purpose of the partnership is to support the parent–child relationship by contributing to parents' understanding of their child and appreciation of their child's uniqueness, reinforcing the importance of the parent in the child's life, and contributing to parents' feelings of competence and confidence.

There must be clarity about the nature and purpose of the relationship. Practitioners in ECE programs sometimes talk about being like close friends or extended family to families of children they work with. Sometimes in ECE programs there is confusion about the differences between friendship and a warm, caring professional relationship. Of course these two kinds of relationships have characteristics in common—warmth, informality, common interests, and enjoyment of each other's company, to name a few. However, thinking that the aim is to become friends with the families of children in the service can cause problems.

These notions actually interfere with a desirable professional relationship rather than support it. Friendship and extended family suggest lifelong connections, which may occur, especially in family child care, but are not a necessary outcome of an effective relationship. They also suggest reciprocity; that is, what I ask you to do for me you have a right to ask of me. How appropriate is it, if you are a family child care provider, that at the end of a difficult day when parents come to pick up their child, you ask them to take your children home with them, give them a meal and a bath, and you will pick them up later—and of course you'd be willing to pay! Friendship and extended family suggest a relationship that lacks boundaries about what can be asked. These dimensions do not fit with a professional relationship. Where personal friendships exist before a parent uses the program or where one develops, the practitioners and parents must try to keep the personal and professional relationships separate.

The notion of treating children as if they are your own is similarly dangerous. Of course, there are some ways in which, especially in family child care, this notion has some validity. However, the passion, lifelong commitment, and relative lack of objectivity that most parents feel about their own children are a special feeling that signifies a deep and close relationship. The best experience for children comes when the commitment and passion that the parent feels is combined with the relative objectivity and dispassionate approach of practitioners.

The real danger in seeing yourself as a substitute parent for children is that it makes it easier to disregard the child's family and culture. It makes it easy to make decisions yourself about the child without consulting them and maybe even without letting them know. The result is that parents are not empowered to contribute to decisions about the child's experience in care and perhaps start to feel less essential to their child. They may not object to your taking over; rather they may go along with it because they trust you and assume that as a professional you know best, because they don't want to rock the boat, or because they don't realize that it could be, should be, different. This situation can also lead to an unhealthy dependence on practitioners by parents. In short, practitioners should treat children as though they are other people's children—which they are!

A related issue is that of being clear about the limits of your professional expertise and the boundaries around the relationship with families. Parents may confide in you about family and personal problems and ask for advice. A tension exists for practitioners between showing compassionate interest in the parents and the whole family and maintaining a focus on the child and on the areas where there is professional expertise.

Confidence

Highlighting the need for confidence in order to work collaboratively with parents does not mean that the practitioner must always be sure that he or she is right. Rather, confidence allows practitioners to admit that they are sure that they are *not* always right, that they make mistakes sometimes, and that there is always something more to learn. This is the kind of confidence that invites other perspectives and ideas, and that is not easily threatened. It is actually lack of real confidence that leads to closed-mindedness, that sees opposing views and difference as a threat, and that is likely to adopt a judgmental approach to diversity.

Confidence is the expression of what might be called optimum certainty. It arises from:

- strongly held beliefs and values on the one hand, and acceptance that other people may hold beliefs and values that may be the opposite of yours on the other;
- perseverance in the face of obstacles and the courage to change directions and admit that a course of action isn't working;
- openness to others' perspectives and a willingness to continue working together when there are differences until a mutually satisfactory solution can be reached; and
- the ability to compromise when differences can't be sorted out, plus clarity about bottom lines and where you won't compromise.

Confidence also leads to openness to diversity, an appreciation that diversity isn't a problem to be solved or an undesirable situation, but rather something that enriches the experience of being in an early childhood program and our lives in general. The confident practitioner appreciates that there are many good ways to rear children, as long as they feel loved and valued for who they are.

Empathy

Collaborating with parents requires putting empathy, or taking the perspective of the other, into action. This doesn't mean that you have to be a parent yourself, but it does mean that you need a well-developed capacity to put yourself in the shoes of others. If you are a practitioner who is also a parent, one of the things that helps the most when you are feeling critical of a parent is to remember some of your own parenting moments when you did or said the wrong thing. No one is able to always do what they know is best. Throw away notions of the perfect parent.

Empathy helps us to keep in mind what it might feel like to be a parent using an early childhood program. Even when it is a wonderful experience, there is still a degree of vulnerability, as it involves exposing your child and your parenting to the scrutiny of practitioners and other parents.

Empathy reminds us that we don't expect children to trust us immediately, and we go to great lengths to give them time and experiences that build trust and security. We must do that with parents also.

Empathy helps with parents who challenge. Some parents are annoying or demanding occasionally, and a few make you really angry. The most difficult parents to form a relationship with are those who are critical of what you do; seem irresponsible, demanding, or uncooperative; and, most particularly, those who do not appear to be caring well for their child. It is the essence of professionalism to work well with parents who are challenging to work with.

Competence

Competence includes a range of skills and sensitivities. Working well with parents takes time, and therefore requires the practitioner to be organized. For example, making brief notes about information to share with parents or issues to discuss ensures the smooth flow of communication. It takes competence to strike a balance between conveying to parents that you know what you are doing, on the one hand, and encouraging parents to contribute advice, information, and suggestions to their child's experience in the program on the other.

A further dimension of competence is making judgments about the relationship with each family, matching your perceptions of their level of confidence and resilience with your interactions with them. For example, you may decide that it is in everyone's best interests to be more tactful and cautious with some parents than with others in sharing concerns about their child.

There are many skills associated with effective communication and professional relationships that competent practitioners have. They include, among many others:

- being an effective listener;
- knowing when to offer advice and when not to;
- providing information and advice in "digestible" chunks without overwhelming families; and
- being honest when discussing difficult issues with parents and at the same time avoiding being devastatingly discouraging.

Competence also means tuning in to others' styles of communicating and relating, understanding that there are both individual and culturally based characteristics that affect relationships, and adjusting interactions and communication to fit individuals.

Connections

It is critical for ECE programs to have strong links with the larger community for at least two reasons:

1. to ensure that families have access to the support that they need; and
2. to give children the opportunity to be part of the local community and to begin to gain a sense of the responsibilities and benefits of constructive citizenship.

It is worth taking stock occasionally of the extent that your program is connected with your community, both the broader geographical community—the grocery store, the library, and service clubs, for example— and the professional community—child health centers, schools, the local government, welfare agencies, other ECE programs, and any organizations or agencies whose business is supporting families with young children. The most effective links are active, vigorous, dynamic, and go far beyond simply having on hand an up-to-date list of agencies and their contact details. These links will assist families to link in to their broader community as well.

Another dimension of connections is the extent to which a culture of collaboration, mutual support, and teamwork exists within a program. This extends to all groups and individuals within the program—management, support staff, families, and children. Collaboration with parents must start from an attitude that extends to all dimensions of the operation

of the program. This culture or attitude translates into policies and procedures, professional development, and other foundations for the daily
work with families.

Commitment

There has to be a strong commitment to the vision of collaboration and
partnership, as it is not achieved effortlessly. This commitment must, of
course, be translated into action, and requires strength to carry it out, especially in the face of obstacles. More important, there is also the issue
of initiative. Responsibility for a collaborative relationship does not rest
equally with parents and practitioners. While parents do have responsibilities to the program, the ball is much more in the practitioner's court.
They must set the stage, persevere in the face of seeming disinterest or
even rejection, and establish an expectation that collaboration is the norm.
Parents using ECE programs may not be sure what to expect, or may not
know what to ask or to comment on.

THE NATURE OF COMMUNICATION

At the risk of belaboring the obvious, it may help to classify some of the
kinds of communication and conversations that practitioners and parents
have in terms of what they achieve for the partnership, particularly in
terms of benefits to parents.

- Conversations that reassure the parents that you value and enjoy
  their child and that you take notice of their child as a unique
  individual. EXAMPLE: *Lauren has a great sense of humor. She is always
  making us laugh.*
- Comments that let parents know that you think their child is
  developing well. EXAMPLE: *Mali has just started pulling herself up to
  standing holding on to things. It's so exciting to see that happening. It
  won't be long before she is walking!*
- Conversations that let parents know that you think their child's
  behavior is typical for the age or stage. EXAMPLE: *You know, Charlie
  is occasionally biting other children. Unfortunately, a lot of 2-year-olds
  do that. Could we talk about what we can do about it together?*
- Insights that give parents information about what lies behind
  their child's behavior. EXAMPLE: *Maybe Sasha would find it easier to
  settle in the mornings if we gave her breakfast here, so that your routine*

at home in the mornings wouldn't be quite so rushed for you and her. Would that help?

- Requests that enlist parents as collaborators in solving problems. EXAMPLE: *Omar doesn't want to wear his hat outside, and we have a policy that all children must wear one. I wonder if we could figure out a way to help him wear the hat.*

- Comments that reinforce to the parent that you aren't competing with them and that they are the most important person in the child's life. EXAMPLE: *What a huge smile Daniel has when he sees you walk in the door. He does so well here, but he sure is glad to see you.*

- Demonstrations of respect for culture and language. EXAMPLE: *Could you tell us more about Ramadan? We have read about it but we would like to know more.*

- Information about aspects of behavior that parents might not otherwise notice or pay attention to. EXAMPLE: *We've noticed how much Amy seems to delight in music. And she has such great rhythm.*

- Signs that you are aware of and respect the family's lifestyle and child rearing practices. EXAMPLE: *We're trying letting Ali fall asleep on a cushion in the play room. He was having trouble going to sleep in the sleep room and we thought that since he is used to sleeping in a room with others this might help.*

- Indications that you appreciate how hard it is to balance work or study and family life. EXAMPLE: *It must be so hard for you to get ready for your exams and look after Amelia.*

- Evidence that you are interested in them as people and in the family. EXAMPLE: *How are the plans for the new house coming along?*

- Reassurance about their parenting. EXAMPLE: *You have such a good way of calming Noel down when he is upset. It seems to work every time.*

That last example particularly is a reminder of an obvious caution: avoid being false or patronizing. Also, parents who use professional ECE programs may feel a bit exposed and under scrutiny at the best of times, so be careful not to give them the impression that their every action is being observed.

You can see from the examples above that the kinds of conversations we are talking about are not startling—rather they are the everyday exchanges that take place in many ECE programs. No doubt you recognized yourself in at least some of those examples given above.

An important piece of general advice for practitioners who want to support families in their child rearing is to take advantage of every opportunity to share with parents good news about their child. Any time you can honestly tell a parent something positive, interesting, amusing, or affirming about their child, our advice is to "just do it." Almost all parents delight in hearing positive comments from others about their child. Go beyond the generic "She had a good day" type of comments.

Discussing Difficult Issues

When practitioners have concerns about a child, the communication with parents needs to be more considered. Timing is everything. The issue may be something that needs to be raised immediately or can wait. So, when should potentially difficult issues be brought up? It depends on the parent and the concern. However, concerns should never be brought up when the child can hear, or when other children or parents are around. To some extent, the practitioner needs to determine when the parent will be most receptive and able to handle the conversation positively, so that means avoiding, if possible, times when the parent seems in a hurry or exhausted. A strong partnership and easy ongoing communication in general provide a healthy foundation for discussing difficult issues.

When discussing a difficult issue it is important to accept the feelings that arise during the discussion. When practitioners are uncomfortable with feelings, they may ignore them or try to make them go away. It's far better to practice good listening skills and hear out the parents if they wish to express their feelings. Sometimes when people are upset they get angry, lash out, and try to blame the other person. Realizing that can happen helps practitioners become aware of their own responses and keep themselves from reacting defensively. Just listening with empathy can help get the feelings out in the open and they may well dissipate. Responding defensively can create an argument and make parents feel that they aren't understood.

Discussing any issue, especially a difficult one, is a challenge when you don't speak the parent's language. Obviously a solution is a translator; however, it is important to find a good one. A story from the medical profession involves a couple refusing to sign a consent form for surgery to save their child's life because the translator kept telling them that their signature would allow the doctor to butcher the child. It wasn't until a different translator was brought in that everyone realized the mistake.

It may seem reasonable to let a child translate to the parents. In general this is not a good idea, especially when discussing a difficult issue and particularly if it concerns the child. For one thing, children don't have the vocabulary or sophistication to translate a serious adult conversation. For another, it puts the child above the parent, which may create authority issues in the family.

COMMUNICATION STRATEGIES

Now for some specific suggestions:

- Consider using strategies such as notebooks, sticky notes, or a portfolio of children's work, but don't place too much emphasis on them; see them as supplements to rather than substitutes for face-to-face communication.
- Find ways of connecting with parents, letting them in on their child's day. Displaying the written plan is a good idea, but go beyond that. Look at how it is written, what language is used, and think about what meaning, if any, a parent would make of it. Every profession has its own jargon, and the early childhood profession is no different. There are many words and phrases that we use that make little or no sense to someone outside the profession. Another issue about displaying written plans for families is that even if the language is clear, often they are written in a kind of code that practitioners understand, but parents may not. It may be useful to actually ask parents what meaning they take from the written information you provide. You may get some surprises!
- Find ways of encouraging parents to share ideas, make suggestions, and contribute to the experiences offered not only to their child but also to all children in the program. Encourage them to let you know about interesting and/or important events in the child's life outside the program.
- Encourage parents to ask questions, make requests, and engage in constructive criticism. When parents make a request or a demand, adopt a "Why not?" stance instead of an immediate "Can't do" position. We're not suggesting that you actually say "Why not?" to the parent, but rather that you ask yourself this question as a way of testing out if you are trying to collaborate with parents. Asking yourself "Why not?" does not always lead to saying yes to their requests. There are many times when a request cannot be granted. The point is to make clear to parents that it is always acceptable to ask the question or make the request; and when the answer is no, it is given respectfully with no condescension or implication that the request itself was improper.
- Find ways to get parents to tell you what they like about the program, what pleases them as well as what they don't like.
- Update with parents the kinds of information that are collected when a child first begins participating: about interests, likes and

dislikes, biggest challenges, favorite things to do, least favorite things to do.

- Offer an opportunity occasionally for parents to have an interview or discussion "not on the run."
- Get tensions and issues out in the open and talk about them. It sometimes seems that we operate in ECE programs with "deep dark secrets," issues we discuss among ourselves but don't share with parents. Some examples of issues that are best out in the open are:

> Children often behave better for other people than they do for their parents. We are more likely to be on our best behavior with people other than the people we are closest to, the ones we know will love us no matter how badly we behave.
>
> Who is responsible for the child when the parent is present in the program? This is a common moment of discomfort or tension when the child is "acting up"; the parent is thinking the practitioner should do something, and the practitioner is wondering why the parent isn't intervening.
>
> Sometimes, often in fact, parents have difficulty separating from their child even when the child is comfortable with it.
>
> It is normal for parents to worry that their child may become more attached to the practitioner than they are to their parents.
>
> Practitioners aren't trying to substitute or take the place of parents.
>
> A toddler who is a committed and skillful biter isn't likely to become a serial killer (or a vampire!) when she or he grows up.
>
> When a child doesn't act like it's a big deal when the parent returns at the end of the day, or worse still resists going home, it doesn't mean he or she likes the early childhood program more than home.

- Don't aim to be a walking child development textbook. Just talk about what you know in a natural way. (Of course, it is also true that the more you know about child development and other areas, the better your conversations will be.)

It's important to understand that working in collaboration with parents does not mean taking on an extra thing, doing something *in addition* to working with children. Almost always when practitioners are asked what is the major obstacle to working closely with parents, their answer is *time*. Sure more time would help—time to be less busy and to *appear* less busy to parents, time for one-to-one discussions and interviews, time to write notes to parents. If you think that time is the main obstacle, then maybe it would be useful to think about what you could do differently *without additional time.*

CONCLUSION

We have to take it as a given that these relationships are either forged or not forged mostly at the edges of the day, at drop-off and pick-up times, admittedly not the ideal times for relaxed conversations and interactions. People who work in early childhood programs have many demands on their time and energy. You may need to remind yourself and your colleagues of the impact they can have on a parent's understanding and appreciation of his or her child. In the final analysis, the best thing we can do for almost all children is to promote a strong sense of connection and belonging with their family; one of the most damaging things is to weaken that sense of belonging and connection.

And, like most things in this life that matter, relationships are not built through cataclysmic monumental encounters, but rather through a mosaic of small, sometimes unconscious, often brief, sometimes seemingly insignificant encounters. Partnerships with families are built through what we say, what we don't say, what we do, what we don't do. There is a line in the lyric of the John Lennon song *Beautiful Boy*: "Life is what happens to you while you're busy making other plans." Truly collaborative relationships with families are a bit like that—they are made or not made in the hustle and bustle of daily life in a busy early childhood program.

LOOKING FORWARD

In the next chapter we focus on the main categories of information that practitioners, working in partnership with families, need to guide their practice.

Note: Some of the material in this chapter is adapted with permission from two booklets written by Anne Stonehouse and published by the Centre for Community Child Health, Royal Children's Hospital Melbourne in 2001. They are *The Heart of Partnership in Family Child Care: Carer–Parent Communication* and *The Cornerstone of Quality in Family Child Care and Child Care Centers: Parent–Professional Partnerships.*

3

Sources of Knowledge, Foundations for Practice

THIS CHAPTER LOOKS AT SOME of the most important things that are worth knowing and taking into consideration in planning children's experiences. The title of this chapter could be "Where do you get the ideas for what you end up doing?" Some of the answers to that question are obvious, but we hope to expand your thinking to include some new considerations, and to remind you of some sources that you actually use but might not identify. We see that there are at least eight main areas to look at. These include:

1. professional knowledge;
2. the child in the context of the family;
3. the aims and philosophy of the program;
4. colleagues;
5. the community;
6. current events;
7. the geographical and environmental context; and
8. yourself.

PROFESSIONAL KNOWLEDGE

There are a number of categories of knowledge that the competent practitioner needs to acquire and update continually. The most important of these is children's development and learning.

Development and Learning

All practitioners need to acquire a deep understanding of the general progression of typical development and learning from birth to 5 years old and beyond. Not only do they need to be able to identify key milestones, but they also must be aware of the significance of aspects of development and their implications for the experiences and opportunities the child is offered. That means adults working with young children need knowledge of the typical interests, characteristics, behaviors, challenges, and issues that are present in most children at different times as they grow.

Development and learning are parts of the same process of the child's physical, mental, and emotional capabilities becoming increasingly more complex, which in turn influences their behavior. The careful observer can see certain changes in activities, thought patterns, language skills, and emotional reactions as children engage with and make meaning of their world. All of these have implications for the child's experience in the early childhood program. Motivation for learning is usually built in to the typically developing child and shows through children's curiosity and constant need to involve themselves with people and things, but adults play a critical role in supporting and extending that learning. Deep and broad knowledge of development enables an adult to do four important things:

1. see typical behaviors in a positive rather than negative light;
2. support the child's learning and development actively;
3. be alert for possible developmental delays; and
4. be excited about and engaged with children.

Seeing Certain Behaviors in a Positive Light. The professional who knows about typical patterns of development is able to see particular behaviors that would otherwise be seen as problems or misbehavior and understand them to be progress rather than the opposite. They can then share this understanding with parents. For example, the baby who used to just lie there grows into an explorer who crawls all over the place, touching everything and even pulling things off shelves, tipping things over and generally making a big mess. When adults recognize this as a typical behavior of the age group, they are more likely to appreciate it and less likely to curb the child's natural inclinations.

As another example, the explorer grows into a toddler who says "no" and runs the other way when you say, "Come here, please." Adults who understand that defiant behavior eventually leads to independence and individuality will expect such behavior. If independence and individuality are desired cultural characteristics, adults are likely to be more tolerant of behaviors that lead to them. They can look at this behavior as progress rather than an indication that something is wrong with the child or the way the family is rearing the child, or that the child is just being "naughty." Understanding the behavior and having the goals of independence and individuality make it more likely that the practitioner will work with the child in ways that promote the goals. If independence and individuality are not family priorities, it is important that the practitioner understands what the priorities are, because the response to the defiant child may be different.

Actively Supporting the Child's Learning and Development. The second reason to be familiar with information about typical patterns of development is that the knowledge enables professionals to provide for what the child needs now, by allowing, encouraging, or planning for experiences that match the child. Seeing and naming the developmental phenomenon is not enough—the professional must also appreciate what it means for the child's engagement with the world and what it says about what the child needs in the environment, interactions, and relationships to support that development.

Knowing about development helps professionals provide encouragement and support to move forward. We're not advocating pushing children from one milestone to the next, but rather anticipating what's next, which leads to adults providing opportunities for the emerging skills to come out as well as providing for what the child is interested in doing right now. For example, if a baby is ready to stand on his feet but has nothing to hang on to, he'll be frustrated. It isn't special equipment that's needed, merely a coffee table, a couch, a bookcase, or a low room divider. That's the sort of thing that aware adults provide. A 4-year-old who is noticing printed words in books and signs may want to try her hand at writing. If there is nothing to write on or with, an opportunity to pursue this interest is lost. We're not saying that 4-year-olds should learn to write. We are saying that some 4-year-olds are inclined to try their own version of writing and, if they are, they need encouragement and opportunities to do so.

Being Alert for Possible Developmental Delays. Some children don't follow the usual developmental and learning progressions. There can be enormous individual differences in timing, even among children with typical development and learning patterns. The differences are of course even greater for children with atypical development and learning patterns. We're not suggesting that anyone constantly compare children to a chart of ages and stages. Yet, having the knowledge of typical developmental and learning progressions, including expectations for the time and order of developing skills and behaviors, may help adults see some warning signs that those who don't have this knowledge may miss. We still want to emphasize individual differences and warn against premature judgments. At the same time, early identification of delays or particular challenges can often lead to doing something helpful about them. This knowledge should be used to help and support children by opening up possibilities rather than putting lowered expectations and therefore constraints on them.

When trying to decide if a child has a delay, it is important to understand the role cultural expectations play. You can't judge what are typical developmental and learning patterns without knowledge of cultural differences. What is important at a young age in one culture may develop sooner than it does in another culture where it is not important until later. For example, in parts of India where children are taught to eat with their right hands and to use the left hand for toileting, 2-year-olds can tell right from left (Rogoff, 1990). That's different from our experience in Australia and the United States, which is that many typically developing children are still having trouble distinguishing right from left when they are 5. An explanation might be that, in India, they need that skill early in life to be social and eat with other people. In our Western countries, learning left and right only becomes important when a child begins to read and write, so what an Indian parent might consider a developmental/learning delay isn't a delay at all in a different cultural context.

Another example of a cultural difference in development comes from a Native American woman who was told that it wasn't developmentally appropriate for 3- to 5-year-old children to sit still for long periods of time. Indeed it is common knowledge among early childhood professionals trained in the traditions of the profession that under-5s are highly active and their attention span is short. However, this Native American woman's experience was different. She explained to one of the authors that when she was a child, she and her peers were not only expected to be still and attentive, but were able to sit quietly for long periods of time. It was important for them to learn the spiritual traditions of her culture, and that was the only way to learn them. Because they were important, everyone knew they needed to be learned young. She worried that because of a different understanding of what children need, her cultural traditions were dying out. She had a very different expectation for young children from that of her child's preschool teacher, whose experience was that children become restless after just a few minutes of sitting.

So, it is important to recognize that the information about developmental and learning progressions needs to be understood as a general overview and not a rigid template. When used with caution, this kind of information can be helpful for understanding behaviors as they appear. Adult expectations of children's behavior are powerful and can actually influence what they are able to do. That fact can both harm children and help them. It is up to us to be sure that our expectations have a positive effect. We need to examine our assumptions and expectations and keep the child and family's best interests at heart at all times.

Increased Rewards from Engagement with Children. The more you know about children in general and about individual children, the more rewarding it is to work with them. There are many important developmental achievements that may go unnoticed unless their significance has been pointed out. For example, most people get excited and take notice when a baby first sits alone, crawls, or pulls up to standing. However, unless you know what it means, you might miss noticing a baby's grasp becoming more deliberate, or the ability to hold an object in each hand at the same time, or the increase in the range of sounds a baby makes. These are significant but much more subtle achievements. Unless you know about the link between showing surprise and cognitive development, you might miss the positive significance of a toddler's negative reaction to your new hairstyle. The rewards are greater when you can celebrate each child's achievements and be a wise observer and supporter of development.

The Limitations of Developmental Expectations

Information about children's development and learning, what to expect of children of different ages and possible cultural variations due to differences in values and priorities, should guide but not dictate what is provided for children. Professional knowledge helps you to understand what you are seeing and hearing when you look at individual children.

Traditionally, there has been great reliance in early childhood programs on practitioners focusing on traditional areas of children's development, often armed with a detailed list of developmental milestones, collecting information about each child's status, and planning specific activities for the group and for individual children in response to that information. Certainly curriculum planning can include observing children's capabilities in traditional areas of development to look for areas of strength and also areas where encouragement may be needed.

Using developmental information as a way of arriving at curriculum is one way, but only one way. There are many other ways to learn about children that should be used alongside taking a good look at children's developmental status. Watching children as they go about their business, listening to them, engaging and talking with them are the best ways to know them. The well-informed thinking practitioner doesn't restrict her- or himself to formal observations or to a focus on developmental milestones, but looks and listens attentively all the time. We also recommend that when you look and listen, you put what you know from studies or books "on the back burner" and just look at the child. That is, don't be constrained by categories or traditional frames for looking at a child. If you watch the child with a strong mind-set about developmental milestones in general or a particular area of development, you are likely to see only what fits with that particular mind-set. Or it may be a cultural lens that you use to observe a particular child, and what you see may be influenced by what you know or believe to be true about cultural differences. Don't throw away lenses and mind-sets, but do be open to what you are actually seeing and hearing. You will learn lots more about the child that way. Of course, even when it's "on the back burner," the more knowledge you have about children in general and the greater the variety of perspectives you are aware of, the more you are likely to see.

The following examples show how openness to possibilities leads to greater wisdom.

> James, a toddler, is having trouble separating from his mom. That observation might be attributed simply to his developmental level, as separation tends to be difficult for children his age. Closer, more open observation reveals that James is only upset if his mom or dad rushes in and rushes out, or if he is left on his own and not taken into a staff member's arms.

> Jamilla, another toddler, suddenly develops a passion for biting. "Typical toddler behavior," the practitioner might say, so the only solution is to try to minimize frustration and be close to her all the time. Closer observation reveals that she bites not when she is frustrated, but only when she gets overly excited, as she often does after vigorous physical activity.

> Daisy is 3 and hungry, but she sits passively in front of her plate with a chicken leg on it and makes no attempt to feed herself. She looks around for an adult to feed her. The practitioner who is thinking of the stages of physical development decides Daisy is developmentally delayed, or alternatively that this is a social-emotional problem: Daisy is overly dependent. Several other factors come into play here, which make the professional's assumptions faulty. Daisy's family puts a priority on interdependence and she is always fed at home, so naturally she expects the same at day care. Daisy has never in her life eaten food that was not accompanied by rice. Daisy has been taught to never touch food with her hands. Daisy is a vegetarian.

Other Areas of Knowledge

Of course, professional knowledge extends far beyond child development. Practitioners need to know about traditional kinds of experiences that are enjoyed by children of different ages—experiences that support their development and learning. Information about the equipment and materials that are necessary to provide those experiences is also a part of that knowledge. The equipment and materials include such things as sand, water and block play, settings and props for dramatic play, open-ended materials that lend themselves to multiple uses, riding toys, construction or manipulative toys, creative art materials, music, opportunities for movement and dance, outdoor space and equipment that encourage the use of the large muscles of the body, that is, arms, legs, and trunk (large motor skills). Most early childhood programs would include these, because over the years, over ages, over settings, they have been shown to be of interest and value to young children. Although cultural priorities may show up as variations in the experiences, equipment, and materials, the general professional knowledge is still valid.

Sources of Professional Knowledge

All ECE programs need leadership from people who have broad and deep knowledge of many areas, including children's development, learning, health, nutrition, and safety; the nature of appropriate experiences for children; cultural issues; and contemporary families. This knowledge can come in part through working directly with children, especially where there is a learning culture among the people working together. A learning culture means that issues are discussed and information is shared. This shared knowledge provides a backdrop or context for learning from the particular children, families, settings, program aims, and philosophies that also inform practice.

A very important source of knowledge is engaging in formal study. It is imperative that a substantial number of people in ECE programs have formal qualifications, and that they are in positions to provide leadership and guidance to those who have less knowledge and fewer skills. Professional knowledge is of course not static, but must be updated continuously, through reading, discussion, and participation in conferences and other forms of professional development.

THE CHILD IN THE CONTEXT OF THE FAMILY

There is increasing recognition and attention to the need to look at each child in the context of family, culture, and community. Rita Warren (1977, p. 8) writes about the inappropriateness of early childhood practitioners operating with the notion that "children spring into being each morning when they come to us and dematerialize at their departure." The child cannot be known and catered to without knowing his or her unique circumstances. Looking at the child in context makes the job of working well with children more complex in some ways, but also makes it much more likely that the child's experience in the early childhood service will be meaningful and will have a lasting positive impact on the child's life.

Children and their families are obvious sources of the curriculum. Chapter 2 was about the collaborative relationship that should exist between practitioners and parents. The children's experience should be the direct outcome of that collaboration. Using parents as a source of curriculum requires doing at least two things simultaneously:

- letting parents in on your ideas, perceptions, plans, concerns, philosophies, and professional values; and
- at the same time, demonstrating to them that you are genuinely interested in knowing what they want for their child, what suggestions they have, what worries or concerns them, and what they can contribute in the way of ideas, resources, time, talents, and assistance.

You have to go beyond simply reporting on the day's events, or displaying the program or plans. Practitioners must truly want to know about parents' ideas and concerns and be committed to taking account of those ideas and concerns and putting them into practice when that is possible. For example, if a parent or group of parents has serious concerns about their children's clothes getting stained or torn because of the wonderfully challenging environment and opportunities you have created, you need to be open to listening to their complaints and figuring out a constructive way of dealing with them.

Wanting to hear about parents' ideas and concerns does not mean always being able to go along with them. There will be many reasons why every request a parent makes cannot be agreed to. That needs to be clear to parents. What also needs to be clear is that you always want to hear what they want, you will give any request consideration, and when it cannot be agreed to, you will explain the reasons to them respectfully and without any implication that making the suggestion or request was inappropriate. We're not saying that you can't figure out ways to respond to this particular concern about clothes. We're also not saying that you have to tone down your interesting environment and restrict messy opportunities. We are saying that you have to figure out together with the parents what to do when they have concerns about your program.

Looking at the child in context means that sometimes you will decide to make adjustments to practice specifically because of the parents' priorities, even when they are different from your own. For example, many years ago one of the authors was involved in a center that had a child placed in it from a family where the father was suspected of child abuse. When this father informed the staff that he wanted the center staff to toilet train his 22-month-old child as soon as possible, the staff initially resisted. This child was very timid and lacked confidence, and furthermore was showing no signs of being interested in learning to use the toilet. However, given the father's insistence and the obvious importance he placed on having his child use the toilet, eventually the staff decided that it was in this child's best interests to learn to use the toilet as quickly as possible. They decided to do whatever they could to make using the toilet a pleasant experience for this child.

As another type of example, in some communities parents are very keen for their child to learn letters and numbers and to begin to read at an early age. Professionals, even those who believe strongly that children in the preschool years should not be pushed to learn these unless they show interest, may in some circumstances decide, if they look at the child in the context of family, community, and culture, that it is important that they find ways to encourage these kinds of learning.

It is challenging for practitioners to take parents' requests seriously when what they want is different from what the practitioner thinks is best. Sometimes parents from particular cultural groups want their children to see themselves as part of the group more than they want them to become independent individuals. When this view is in direct contrast to what practitioners from a different cultural group regard as good early childhood practice, it may be hard to accept both views as valid because they seem to contradict each other.

Using parents' talents and resources and incorporating them into the fabric of children's experience enriches the program and contributes to parents' feelings of contributing to their child's childhood and to the program. Truly empowering parents to work with children alongside professionals requires that professionals let parents in on the conventions of working with children that govern the professional's practice. There is nothing more disempowering than being told after the fact that "that isn't the way we say it" or "this is the way we do it."

Probably the best way to convince parents that you mean business about wanting their input is to let them live it every day in your program. Let them see you incorporating others' ideas, inviting sharing about their child's experience and interests, and let them experience working alongside you. Of course, this may mean that the professional has to let go of some ideas about exactly how things should be done, but that is a small price to pay for working in collaboration. The professional has to be clear about areas where there can be no compromises—for example, harming children in any way—and ensure that parents know about these. We all have tendencies to be ethnocentric and see our way as the only way. One mark of a true professional is the ability to open up to alternative perspectives and suspend assumptions that everyone thinks as he or she does.

Obviously, practitioners who work with groups of children, even small groups such as in family child care, have to find ways to take the individual priorities and preferences of each family and put together an experience that works for all. Parents need to appreciate this challenge that practitioners face, and at the same time practitioners need to accept that parents have their own child's well-being and interests most at heart and will focus mainly on them.

AIMS AND PHILOSOPHY

In addition, the aims and philosophy of the program impact what is offered to children. By aims we are thinking of the purposes or goals of the program. The philosophy is the statement of main values or principles that form the foundation for how the program operates. Aims and philosophies have to be compatible, of course, but different philosophies and aims can go together. As an example, an aim for a program could be to help children be ready for formal schooling. In one program this aim might be supported with a philosophy that values play, cooperation, creativity, children's initiative, and an open structure that encourages resilience, confidence, and autonomy. In fact, we can imagine a statement of philosophy that contains those words. Another program might have the same aim but adopt a philosophy that explicitly values supporting children to achieve in school-related subject areas and to excel through competition and carefully planned and structured experiences in reading, writing, and math.

Aims and philosophies can come from various sources. For example, one service starts as a Montessori program and follows a particular version of that philosophy. The aims of the service fit with the philosophy. That means the general professional knowledge of those who work in the service as well as what is known about the particular group of children, parents, and the community context are combined with the philosophy of the program. An important thing to keep in mind is that when families choose a program because of its philosophy, it is a different situation from if the families don't consider that they have any other choice. In the first situation, the professional's job is to help the families better understand the philosophy they have chosen while still, of course, being responsive to their particular aims and philosophies. In this situation, the program's philosophy remains solid and families are expected to conform to some extent. In the second situation, when the family ends up in a program without any choice in the matter, the aims of the program and its philosophy must be highly responsive to the aims and philosophies of the families involved. Philosophy statements and goals that aren't flexible can be a problem, because of the need to consider the families' priorities and preferences to a greater extent than in the first situation.

It's not easy to be responsive when you have strong ideas, beliefs, and values, while in addition having to comply with a set of standards or regulations about what is good and right for all children, and the families involved also have different ideas. Although differences in ideas and priorities may present challenges, that's what honoring diversity is all about. As children watch adults in their lives grapple with hard questions related to differences in perspectives, they are gaining useful experiences for their lives as citizens in a diverse society.

We have discussed more than once the issues involved with honoring diversity, even when you are uncomfortable about some practices or don't agree. We don't mean that families can have complete freedom to dictate practices and that the professional may be expected to cast aside everything he or she believes in. We do mean that there must be a lot of discussion about philosophy and aims. Those discussions should take place with a spirit of genuine commitment to collaboration. The practitioner can't just read and explain the philosophy with the purpose of convincing the family to go along with it. If a family chose the particular service because of its philosophy and it turns out the philosophy doesn't fit, it makes sense for either the parent or the practitioner to acknowledge the problem and not regard it as failure on anyone's part. If the family leaves after attempts to work through the problems, that's okay. They can look for another service that makes a better fit. That same solution is less acceptable when the parent has no option to choose a different service. In that case, the practitioner should be wary of saying, "Well, that's the way our program is and if it doesn't fit your needs, you should leave." It's up to both the family and the practitioner to figure out how to make the program fit without anyone giving up what they strongly believe in. That type of problem solving is the key to culturally sensitive care.

While there will, of course, be some variation in aims and philosophy from program to program, we believe that all of them should include respect for children and families, appreciation of the importance of the early years for laying the foundations for later development and learning, the need for professionals to work in collaboration with families, and an honoring of diversity. Of course, if honoring diversity appears in a statement of philosophy and is taken seriously, then professionals will necessarily be somewhat flexible and responsive to the wishes and priorities of families.

COLLEAGUES

The people you work with are a terrific source of both inspiration and information to inform practice. Each professional brings unique experience, perspectives, talents, hobbies, and interests to the task of working with children. Services that are vibrant learning communities capitalize on this and create a culture of sharing, dialogue, and constructive critique. It is critical for all professionals to talk with colleagues, to observe their work and to let them observe yours, and to expose yourself to both affirming experiences and ones that confront and challenge. To do this constructively of course requires confidence in yourself and your colleagues, and a culture of cooperation and collaboration rather than competition.

Colleagues can be especially valuable when you are able to connect with those whose programs, background, and training differ from yours. Crossing cultures can be an enriching experience, especially if individuals or groups of professionals are able to talk about differences. What creates barriers is when standards, best practices, and regulations are used to evaluate differences. Sometimes, in the name of being professional, those who have assimilated into the dominant culture and/or the early childhood culture leave behind their diverse ideas and take up the banner of early childhood. Only through developing personal relationships can the discussion go deeper, as both parties begin to feel secure enough to dig deep into their past and upbringing. Learning to talk across cultures with colleagues is good practice for relating across cultures with families.

THE COMMUNITY

The term *community* applies at many levels. First, there is the *community* that is the children's program. There will be a formally stated purpose and philosophy for the program and, in addition, there will be expectations from the people involved in the program. These come to some extent from the formal purpose, and also from traditions, reputation, and the priorities of the practitioners and managers of the program.

In addition, there is the local community where the program resides, which may or may not be the community of most of the families in the program. The greater society can also be looked at as a community, and there are general community expectations of programs that come from history and tradition.

Expectations

Community expectations for the ECE program have to influence curriculum. These expectations may be culturally based, influenced by socioeconomic level, or arise from the policy and funding context for the program. For example, an indigenous community may have strong ideas about children retaining and valuing traditional culture. As another example, the community may be a religious community with strong views about both the celebration and non-celebration of holidays, or the type of stories and literature used with the children.

Professionals both reflect and influence expectations in their practice. They are advocates for children and for good practice. At the same time, they must seriously take into account what the near community and the broader community want and expect. For example, if a religious community believes that children are born into sin and must be led out of it with a strong hand, the practices of that community may go against the grain of the early childhood educator who believes that children are basically good and need freedom to grow and develop. Say this particular community sees play, freedom of interaction, and exploration as too loose for children. The community members instead prefer strict rules that govern every action of the day. Accompanying the rules is constant adult surveillance to enforce them and swift and strict punishment when needed. In this case, many practices in this community are influenced by their belief about the basic nature of the child and those practices are a contradiction to good early childhood practice. If they are looked at by the professional as "bad practice," the ability to discuss them further and understand them becomes blocked. Somehow professionals have to hang on to their own professional ideals as well as be open to different perspectives. To do that, professionals must accept that views other than their own have validity for those who hold them.

Another example of a value contradictory to early childhood practice comes from a community that sees conformity to the group as the primary goal. That community uses only criticism to guide children's behavior and never uses praise. That may seem to tear down children's self-esteem from the professional's view, but the community sees self-esteem as coming from the group, not the individual. Another practice of this community is also in contradiction with early childhood practice. The worst punishment in this community is shunning; that is, cutting the individual off from the group. They regard the early childhood practice of time-out as far too extreme to use with young children. Professionals can't merely disregard ideas and practices of communities they serve, even if they find them opposed to what they believe. Here again, dialogue, discussion, and understanding are called for.

Linking Children and Families with the Community

Getting over these hurdles related to diversity is one aspect of relating to the community, but another is linking children and families into the community. So it isn't just discussion that is needed, but actually taking the children out into the community and bringing the community in. Excursions and visitors are two obvious ways of doing this linking. One program regularly looked for musicians residing in their community and had them come in to play for the children and conduct sing-along group times. Certainly if there are artists and/or craftspeople nearby, they can contribute a lot to the program. Another program went once a month to a parent's workplace, exposing the children not only to the community, but also to the jobs in it. Having community workers such as firefighters and police officers in to talk about their jobs is a time-honored early childhood experience. Even better is visiting them at work. Of course, links with the community are more meaningful to children when they happen more than once, and when they are linked to what is happening in the program.

CURRENT EVENTS

Both what is happening in individual children's lives and what is happening in the broader community must be taken into account, and these can provide a rich source of curriculum. Children's individual lives are marked sometimes with events of great moment, sometimes joyful, sometimes mixed, sometimes sad, frightening, or tragic. Moving to a new home, gaining a new brother or sister, losing a pet, parents separating, the death of a family member, an impending holiday, domestic violence—none of these is out of bounds to deal with in an ECE program. Of course, how they are dealt with, and whether they are dealt with only in response to the child's initiation, are matters for careful professional judgment with parent input. It may seem surprising that death, loss, tragedy, or violence could become part of the curriculum. We mention them because we worry about programs that are so sanitized that they seem irrelevant to the children and families. If we make everything fun all the time, we run the risk of our programs seeming like a day in Disneyland—wonderful, but a day outside of real life. It is critical that what happens to children in ECE programs is relevant and links to their world at home and also the one outside the program. If it doesn't, there is a danger that it might be written off as unconnected, meaningless, or frivolous.

As a small example, when the street repairs outside the window are much more interesting than anything going on inside, it doesn't make sense to stick to the plan and ignore the item of interest just outside. A bigger example occurs when a tragic incident affects everyone in the community. If life in the ECE program goes on as usual, ignoring the children's feelings, fears, questions, and lack of information, it doesn't make sense. In that case, dealing with their feelings, fears, and understanding of the situation becomes the curriculum of the moment.

We don't mean to imply that what happens in the program necessarily mimics or mirrors what is happening outside. For example, sometimes

with major holidays there is a feeling that perhaps children are being satu-
rated with them outside, anticipation building, so that what is needed is
some relief from the build-up. Being aware of what's going on outside allows the practitioner to create a balance. However, whether it is the Olympics, the weather, a natural disaster near or far, or a major cultural event,
there should be appropriate acknowledgment. This may range from a major focus to simply acknowledgment and responding to children's questions and interest.

GEOGRAPHICAL AND ENVIRONMENTAL CONTEXT

Obviously each program happens in a particular environmental context:
city, suburban, rural, remote, cold, hot, rainy, dry, coast, hills, desert. Every environment offers opportunities for children to learn, explore, and
feel a part of where they are. One of the aims of an early childhood program is to nurture in children a love of nature, and a desire to preserve,
protect, and enhance the natural world around them. We referred to the
"packaged curriculum" in the first chapter in this book. These prepack-
aged curricula inevitably include the seasons, but often the portrayal of
the seasons is totally inappropriate for the location of the program. One
example is "doing winter" with snowflakes, ice skating, and skiing in
a subtropical climate. Another example is of a practitioner doing group
time in July around "What animals like winter?" She shows the children
pictures of polar bears, while outside it is a mild day and there's a field
nearby probably full of local animals doing what they do in winter, but
all that is totally unacknowledged.

YOURSELF

Each of us brings our personal experience and qualities to our understanding of children and families. Understanding your own assumptions,
perspectives, blind spots, and biases and how they impact on your work
is part of your job. Self-knowledge is important when relating to children
and their families.

Every practitioner also brings particular strengths, talents, and interests, both personal and professional, to their work. Knowing what
these are and figuring out how they can be used on behalf of the children
and families is rewarding for the individual and enriching for the program, even, or perhaps especially, when they are not part of the usual
repertoire of traditional early childhood programs. One of the authors

knew a teacher who loved rocks, and she helped children learn to love rocks through demonstrating her passion for them. Another example is a friend of one of the authors who is an early childhood professional and also an accomplished belly dancer. The children enjoy belly dancing, and the dressing up that goes with it, and some of them have become very skilled at it.

CONCLUSION

To work effectively with children we must know them. We must know them as a group and as individuals. Not only must we know children, but we must also know their families and the communities the families belong to. Further, we must know ourselves. Only when we bring all these and other areas of knowledge together can we work in partnership with parents and families to provide the very best experiences for each child.

It's an early childhood cliché that what happens in an early childhood program should arise out of children's needs and interests. No doubt all early childhood practitioners believe that and act on it to some extent. And yet we might ask how, if this is so, can packaged curricula be so popular, and how is it possible to respond to children's interests and plan the curriculum months in advance? In this chapter we reminded you of some of the sources of ideas and inspiration for what you do with children.

Creating curricula by bringing to bear all the knowledge discussed in this chapter is complex. We acknowledge also that many factors restrict or constrain what can be offered in ECE programs. Lack of time, inadequate resources, constantly shifting groups of children, insufficient numbers of staff or insufficiently qualified staff, and staff turnover are just a few. A major constraint may be that the requirements for thinking and creativity in taking the approach advocated in this book may be daunting to some. That is, a packaged curriculum might seem much easier. We challenge you to move beyond your fears and try what we recommend.

LOOKING FORWARD

While this chapter gave an overview of a number of broad categories of information and knowledge that guide practice, the key to excellence is bringing all of those areas to understanding and planning for individual children. The next chapter, a very long one, is the heart of this book, and builds on what has come before, particularly the discussions of general knowledge and the child in context that began this chapter.

4

What's Worth Knowing About Each Child

I N ADDITION TO KNOWING ABOUT CHILDREN in general and their development, practitioners need to learn about each child as an individual. But remember the child is never a stand-alone individual; each comes to an ECE program from a family and community context, and it's quite likely that at times the individual family or the community may not fit patterns that are familiar to the individual practitioner.

Each of us also brings our personal experience to our understanding of children and families. Understanding your own assumptions, perspectives, blind spots, and biases, and how they impact on your work, is part of your job. Self-knowledge is important.

There are some things you want to know about the child in context at the beginning or early in the child's participation. This is information you update continuously. The information you want from an interview at the time of enrollment and from early observations includes:

- the child's abilities in traditional areas of development;
- health (including past major medical conditions);
- family situation;
- past experience of child care or other ECE programs;
- concurrent use of other services (early childhood and others);
- temperament and style;
- strengths, interests;
- parents' priorities and expectations;
- parents' concerns;
- parents' attitudes toward using the service; and
- cultural context of the child's and family's life.

You also need to know about the child's ongoing experience in the program. Pay attention to the fit of the child with the program and the program with the child. Watch and listen for and discuss with parents the following:

- who the child relates to best in the environment;
- the child's favorite parts of the environment;
- the child's favorite experiences;
- the child's overall experience of the program;
- the children the child is drawn to in the program;
- other children's attitudes toward the child;
- how the child settles in upon arrival;
- how the child reacts when the parent leaves and returns; and
- the child's degree of self-control.

As you get to know the parents better, you also want to find out:

- the parents' dreams for the child;
- the parents' confidence level about their parenting; and
- the parents' confidence level about the program.

INTRODUCTION TO OUR ABCs OF KNOWLEDGE

What follows are more details on the above, plus some other information you need about each child. Faced with a large amount of information, we decided to create the ABCs of knowledge as a means of organizing. So, we will discuss 26 different areas of knowledge—one for each letter of the alphabet. Dividing them up this way isn't meant to make this a reference section; that is, we don't expect you to just look up a particular topic. In order to get the full picture, you need to take in the whole alphabet.

Some of the ways we classified information will be familiar, but we also have our own unique perspective. This isn't the definitive alphabet. We thought of many alternatives for most letters. But choosing one concept for each letter is our way of laying out some of what's important and helping you remember it. You can even use this alphabet as a device for checking that you have covered the important things to know. We see this chapter being used to trigger thinking and perhaps structure discussions. You may want to choose one concept at a time as a focus for reflection and discussion with colleagues. It could also be the basis for specialized assessment checklists developed collaboratively with practitioners and parents.

Another important thing to say is that we haven't discussed any of the concepts in a comprehensive way, but rather have made a few selected comments that we think are important. We could write a whole book about each of the 26 areas of knowledge—in fact, books have been written about many of them individually. You will need to see this discussion as adding to your core knowledge about children.

For each letter we explain briefly the concept or concepts behind the word or phrase and put the ideas into some kind of context that shows our perspectives. We assume you have the specific knowledge all practitioners should have, such as information about developmental progression and age-appropriate behavior. If you don't have that knowledge, you need to find some materials on behavior and development and study them along with this book.

Questions for Reflection

We also include lists of questions and suggestions for reflection that you can use to go deeper in your knowledge of the child, his or her family, and yourself. Understanding your own reactions, perspectives, and cultural values is an important part of relating to children and families. When you bump into something that triggers a memory, a feeling, or a surprising response, take it as a sign you need to go further. Sometimes it's much easier to focus outwardly than to look inside. But self-reflection is an important part of being an early childhood professional, and that's why we included it here. You'll find lots of opportunities in the following pages to focus on yourself.

Gender Differences

As we were writing, gender became an issue. Just as we don't want to talk about "the child" as some kind of universal creature with no culture, family, or community, we don't want to talk about children as genderless. For that reason we give each of our examples a gender. That approach serves several purposes. It released us from writing "he or she" each time we talked about a child. It also lets us ask you throughout to reflect on whether gender makes a difference to what you think. If it does, ask yourself if gender makes a difference in reality or if your decision that it does is based on possible misconceptions and biases that you have. To answer that question you may have to dig up the latest research and talk to the people you work with!

Age and Ability Differences

We also didn't want the child to be ageless. Age makes a huge difference. Remember we are writing about children from birth to 5 years.

Infants and toddlers aren't just added as an afterthought—rather they are integrated into the whole book. Also, children with specific challenges, such as those with disabilities, are included throughout, not just put into a special section. They do have their own letter of the alphabet as well, as does culture.

Implications for Practice

Although we have a section at the end of each letter that looks at implications for practice, sometimes the discussion that precedes that section is a mix of what's worth knowing and what you should do about it. *Knowing* is not worth much unless it translates into wise action. Wise action doesn't mean never taking a risk, always taking the safe and sure path. We don't want practitioners to ever put children in unsafe situations, but we do want to encourage you to allow yourself to make mistakes and take reasonable risks. You can learn from those, even when they don't work out. We will give you some ideas about practical applications, some of them riskier than others.

ATTACHMENT

Attachment is a lasting emotional connection, and that connection is the basis for solid growth, development, and learning. Most children who enter an ECE program arrive firmly attached to their families or at least to one person in their family. Usually the attachment is to the mother, although there are many exceptions. Fathers are sometimes as closely attached or more so than mothers. In extended families and kinship networks where there are multiple caregivers, it's not so easy to predict to whom the child will attach. Sometimes it is to several people, one of whom may be a sibling, the grandmother, or another extended family member.

Recognizing the attachment behaviors of each child is usually easy. Babies smile at, hug, and cling more to those to whom they are attached. Older children show interest and affection in a variety of ways. Attachment behaviors are usually easy to see when the parent or family member drops the child off and then leaves. Many children cling, protest, or cry; yet some attached children never show distress. Attachment behaviors are related to age, temperament, and previous experiences.

Think of a particular girl who is about 9 months old. What is worth knowing about this particular child's attachment? Here are some questions to help you:

- What attachment behaviors do you notice?
- Are you aware of differences in attachment behaviors due to developmental or physical challenges?
- Are you aware of attachment behaviors that relate to cultural background?

If your experience is with children of your own culture and children whose development follows typical patterns, you may need to broaden your knowledge and sharpen your observation skills. For example, children with particular developmental or physical challenges may show attachment through different means. A child with cerebral palsy may be exhibiting attachment behaviors that aren't recognized by adults. A smile may look like a grimace. A child with severe visual impairment is not likely to use eye contact as a way of establishing closeness. In these cases, it is very important that practitioners understand the differences and look for signs of attachment that may be overlooked.

There may be cultural differences in attachment behaviors as well. Although eye contact may be considered essential for attachment by people from some cultures, that particular way of making human connections is not universal. What some consider the classic pattern of maternal attachment may be nonexistent in cultures where shared caregiving is the norm or where extended family is the unit rather than parents and children.

Now think about to whom this child is attached and answer these questions:

- How close does this child feel to which family members? This can be useful information as you come to understand the relationships in the family. In some families, other relatives are as important as parents.
- How do those family members respond to the child's attachment behaviors?
- What is the child's relationship to elders in the family?
- What is your relationship to elders in the family? If there are lines of authority in the family that dictate who makes the decisions and with whom you are to communicate, it's important that you know about them.

While you are trying to understand how attachment works with this particular child and family, also consider:

- Can you see some indications of attachment between you and the child? Does the child exhibit attachment behaviors toward you?

Do you have feelings for the child that indicate attachment?
- How do you feel about the family?
- Do you have particular issues yourself around attachment? Consider your own early experiences and your experiences now.
- Is there a particular age child or type of child you are more likely to become attached to? Are you more likely to become attached to boys than girls?

Looking at Gender and Age Differences

Now we want you to change the girl to a boy and go through the questions again. Then we want you to change the child's age and go through the questions again. Continue until you have considered both genders and all ages (in 1-year intervals) from birth to 5. Alternatively, if you are already working in an ECE program, just focus on the gender and ages of the children you work with. Then we want you to think about how big a difference gender made when you answered the questions. Reflect on whether you have different expectations for boys than girls. Do your expectations relate to age or do you expect the same from all children?

There are no right or wrong answers to these questions. Their purpose is not to give you a grade, but rather to help you increase your knowledge in specific areas and to expand your self-awareness. This book and these exercises are designed to improve practice through reflection and dialogue, not by assessing your compliance with standards and regulations.

Implications for Practice

What you learn about the child, the family, and yourself affects what you do. The most immediate and compelling matter is to help and support each child who has problems separating when left in the program. The coping skills the child learns in ECE programs while coming to trust that he or she is not abandoned can last a lifetime. You can provide support and reassurance while helping the child to connect to the toys and materials, to other children and, most important, to you. You have to learn what works with each child. Some don't want you close, but will eventually become interested in something in the environment. Others will cling to you. Others will cling to something they brought from home.

It is important that the child, especially an infant or toddler, develops a feeling of attachment and a sense of belonging over time to at least one person in the program. That someone is usually an adult, although the child may enjoy peer connections as well. It's the practitioner's responsibility to promote attachment when it doesn't seem to be occurring naturally. How that responsibility is carried out in practice has to do with all the ways the practitioner works on relationships during everything that happens every day. It boils down to interactions, which comes up further along in this chapter.

Attachment to other people's children can be a delicate matter. The goal is to become attached, but with enough distance so you don't create unhealthy dependence and/or an expectation of a permanent relationship. You must not see yourself as a substitute for the parent. It's important to become aware of your feelings about and relationship to the family. Although you don't necessarily need to feel a close connection to the family to work well with them, you do need a strong respectful relationship of collaboration and partnership with them.

Although it is rare, you may come across a child whose attachments are weak or nonexistent. If the child is an infant, one of the signs of a weak attachment or lack of one is something called "failure to thrive." Some babies, for no physical reason, don't gain weight or grow normally. Development may be slowed or stopped. "Failure to thrive" is a rather drastic indication of something wrong. However, young children can be damaged by lack of attachment without showing such dramatic signs. The latest brain research indicates the extreme importance of attachment in the early years to healthy growth and to cognitive functions. The architecture of the brain is determined early, and a healthy attachment influences the physical structures the brain ends up with. When you are concerned about attachment issues in any child in your care, no matter what age, start by finding out if the family is also concerned before sharing your perceptions with them. If they are also worried, putting your heads together may help you figure out what to do about the issue. Sometimes, if the problem isn't obvious to the family but turns out to be a true problem, outside help may be needed.

A last word about attachment is about its link to discipline and guidance. Having a relationship with a child is the most effective way to guide behavior, so you should always keep that in mind when choosing discipline approaches. The message (spoken or unspoken) should always be "I am concerned about your behavior because I care about you." Also, whenever possible, avoid doing anything that harms the relationship you have with the child.

BODY

We're not talking in this section about what you need to know about individual children to become a personal trainer. This isn't just about physical education; it's a lot bigger than that and encompasses bodily functions, health issues, and also how the body and mind are connected when it comes to learning. Think about a particular boy. Make that boy 2 years old. Think about what you need to know about the body of this boy. You should learn early on from the family about:

- the health history of the child;
- any current health issues;
- the family's attitudes toward, beliefs about, and perceptions of the child's body; and
- the child's attitudes toward, beliefs about, and perceptions of his body.

You also want to know how the child uses his body; what skills the child has, what skills are lacking. Physical skills are important, but there is also a vital connection between the body and mind. In the early years, children learn with their bodies. All the playing, exploring, and handling of toys and materials they do contributes to their mental skills. They aren't just getting ready to learn, they are learning as they play. Outdoor time, when children have room to stretch their muscles and test their ability to run and climb, is a great time for learning, because learning occurs during those physical actions. Abstract thinking has its basis in the concrete world, so young children need plenty of experience exploring with their bodies. Ask yourself what you know about this particular child's:

- large muscle skills (those of the arms, legs, and trunk);
- level of confidence in using large muscle skills;
- small muscle skills (those of the hand and fingers);
- level of confidence in using small muscle skills;
- eye–hand coordination;
- level of confidence in using eye–hand coordination; and
- ability to coordinate other senses with the hands (especially in the case of a child with visual impairments).

Bodily *functions* are also the concern of early childhood educators. Older children in school take care of their own needs before and after school as well as at recess or between classes and at lunch. The younger the child, the more you need to focus on bodily functions. In the case of a child with physical or other disabilities, bodily functions may be the concern of the practitioner the whole time the child is in the program and may call for specialized skills in taking care of them, such as care of a feeding tube, for example. So what do you need to know about the bodily functions and physical care of each child? Take a look at the caregiving routines, or as they are sometimes called, essential activities of daily living.

Think again about the 2-year-old boy and consider:

- food preferences;
- dietary requirements and restrictions;
- food sensitivities and allergies;
- food and eating patterns, including how much he eats, when, and how;
- family beliefs, attitudes, taboos, and/or rituals around food and eating;
- how the family handles elimination (such as diaper changing and toilet learning) and expects you to;
- the way the child usually goes to sleep;
- washing and grooming procedures or rituals; and
- whether or not the child has physical or developmental differences that influence caregiving routines.

Much can be learned through observation, but also from the parents and/or other family members you're in contact with. Cultural issues may arise around food, eating, and feeding. Dietary beliefs and restrictions can be extremely important matters and must be discussed with families. Understanding and acknowledging your own preferences and beliefs is important too. Then there are regulatory agencies' requirements and standards to consider, some of which have to do with sanitation procedures.

Feeding is everybody's business! Knowing how to feed children safely is vital. Eating in ECE programs is different from eating at home where the family may have similar immunities. Sanitation becomes vital as children are exposed to a wider variety of germs than they have encountered in their own homes. Families may not abide by the same standards. This may be only one area of difference, and many others may exist around feeding practices. Figuring out how to reconcile differences between your practices and the parents' while upholding standards can be an important challenge in the area of feeding and eating.

Diaper changing and toileting, particularly when to start toilet training or learning and how to do it, are areas where the family's ideas may differ from yours and the regulations. Ideas about sleeping, washing, and grooming may also differ.

Looking at Gender and Age Differences

Now we want you to change the boy into a girl and go through the questions again. Then we want you to change the child's age and go through the questions one more time. Change the gender of a child that age and go through the questions again. Continue until you have considered all ages in the range of birth to 5 or the range in your group if it's narrower than birth to 5. Did gender make a difference when you answered the questions? Reflect on whether you have different expectations for boys than girls. Whether gender makes a difference or not, obviously age does. Feeding issues for 6-month-olds are different from those of 5-year-olds, to take a wide extreme.

Toileting also can connect with age. The subject of when to start toilet training comes up when someone considers the child "ready." Do your ideas match with parents' ideas about when children are ready to use the toilet? What about children with disabilities or other kinds of developmental differences? Who decides when they are ready if they don't match anyone's concept of a timetable for readiness? Remember our purpose is not to grade you on right answers, but rather to help you increase your consciousness of differences in children and families to expand your self-awareness. We're not suggesting setting aside standards or regulations. We are asking you to look closely at how you can uphold them, be true to yourself, do a good job of caring for and educating young children, and at the same time be responsive to parents. The book and these exercises are designed to integrate what you know and believe with what you do.

Implications for Practice

What you know about each child's bodily functioning and physical development guides your practice by making you responsive to differences of all sorts—individual, family, cultural, as well as gender and age differences. Setting up an environment for caregiving, exploring, learning, and development depends a good deal on who the children are within that environment. If some of the children have particular physical or developmental challenges, that makes a difference too. The environment should be designed for all the children in it without exception. That means it will change as children develop and as children leave and enter the group.

Interactions during the essential activities of daily living need special attention. Diaper changing is a one-to-one interaction and should be thought of that way rather than as a task. If treated as an interaction or series of interactions, diaper changing can be a time for important learning. It is a time for strengthening relationships, and from strong relationships comes more learning. Approaching these intimate times as a human-to-human contact instead of a job to get done makes all the difference. Feeding infants has the same potential of strengthening relationships if carried out as an intimate act instead of a duty. Not just infants but older children can also find meals a time to strengthen relationships, enjoy as a social occasion, and satisfy hunger while fulfilling nutritional needs.

CULTURE

What do you need to know about each family's culture? Trying to find out information about cultural background can be a delicate process. Understanding a wide variety of cultural differences can be a challenge; after all, some anthropologists study for years to become knowledgeable about one culture. Nobody is asking you to become an anthropologist, but we are asking you to be aware and sensitive to each family in your program. Some families identify their culture openly and immediately and seem eager to share it with you. It may be that they have specific dietary preferences or requirements, so they want you to know straight away what they are. For example, if a family never eats pork or is rearing their child as a vegetarian, it's very important for you to know that. You also need other specifics about what is acceptable and what is not. If the family tells you about their culture, it may be that they are concerned about their child's cultural identity and want your support to affirm it.

When families don't come forth with cultural information on their own, it can be a more complex situation. It may help for you to know how they identify themselves. You may wonder if they perceive differences between their culture and yours (or that of the program). Asking directly when you don't know a family well isn't always the best way to find out. Some people are deeply offended when asked about their culture. They may feel that you singled them out because of the way they look, dress, talk, or the color of their skin. This singling out is especially painful if there are people in the community who are not asked about their culture because either someone makes a false assumption that they don't have one (!) or feels that it is not important to know about it. Often the dominant culture is considered the universal standard so only "other people," those whose cultural background is not the dominant one, are "different." This attitude shows a lack of understanding about cultural awareness.

We can't see our own culture very well unless it bumps up against someone else's. Also, there is enormous institutional power that goes with membership in the dominant culture, including the ability to define what is "normal." It's hard to see that one has a particular cultural perspective when that particular perspective has institutional backing and is considered to encompass everyone.

Instead of asking "What's your culture?", it's safer to work quietly at discovering if a particular family has certain ways they want things done for and with their children. Culture matters, but discovering and understanding similarities and differences is an ongoing project and can get off to a bad start if someone becomes offended by the wrong questions at the beginning. The goal is to build a relationship, and if asking questions that hurt gets in the way of that, it's better to avoid them.

What does it matter if there are cultural or familial differences? Will those affect the way the program runs? Will you do things differently? The degree to which you should be responsive to differences depends on the circumstances, including the family's goals and needs. If families come to this particular program because of its specific identified philosophy, they may be choosing to downplay their cultural or familial differences. Some families are clear that cultural matters are the business of the home and that they want the children's program to have a different set of priorities. For example, families who come to a country for a year or so and are planning to return home may see the period as a chance for their children to experience another culture; they may regard your ECE program as the place to do that. Exchange students and academics who bring their families with them are examples of people in that category. They are making a clear choice. But if families have no choice and end up at the program because it was the only one available with room for their child, then cultural sensitivity and responsiveness on the part of the practitioner may be very important. Even when families have a choice, they have the right to expect that in any program their culture, language, and religious background will be respected.

Immigrants who have chosen to move permanently to another country may be more anxious that their children fit in to the new culture than remain part of the old. The same may be true for families with indigenous roots. Even if a family wants the child to experience a different culture, the practitioner still needs to have a great deal of sensitivity and some knowledge about the child's past and current experience at home. If the parent's goal is for the child to give up the home language and culture for total assimilation into the new culture, the practitioner needs to be sure that the family understands the implications of aiming for that goal. Fitting in without cutting off roots is an alternative and can result in a bicultural child.

Some families value assimilation while other families may have the opposite perspective on what they want from an ECE program. Consider refugees who had no choice, ended up in another country, and have no desire to give up their culture or to take on a new one. Think of immigrant families who are trying to preserve their home culture. Most indigenous people feel strong ties to their cultural roots and want to either keep them or get them back. These groups may see the program as a threat to their children's identity and family cohesiveness.

One of the worst things a program can do is to separate children from their family. Taking on a new culture should be an additive process, not a subtractive one, but it often works the opposite way. Many children turn their backs on the old culture when they embrace the new one. When that happens, they take huge psychological steps away from their families.

They may become disconnected from their people, which has enormous implications for their identity, sense of security, and the family's authority. Discipline issues become huge when children no longer respect or admire their parents because of cultural differences. Worse, when they take on the new language, they may lose the old, so they can't even communicate with their parents. This situation is a tragedy. It's a big responsibility for ECE programs to keep this disconnection from happening. Awareness of the fact that a risk exists for some children to turn their backs on their home language and culture is the first line of defense against it happening.

So, what do you need to know about a family's culture if it is different from yours or from the one that most influences the way you run your ECE program? You need to know:

- if the family is concerned about their child maintaining his or her cultural identity while in your program;
- if the family is comfortable with their child being exposed to a different culture from the home one;
- what language(s) their child speaks and, if they are different from the main one in the program, how they feel about the child being exposed to a language different from the home language;
- what kind of support for their home language and culture they want to have (if any); and
- if the family is making decisions about language and culture from an informed or privileged position of power or if they are making the decisions out of desperation because they are disempowered and don't see any other choice.

Think about a 4-year-old girl in a cross-cultural situation. Ask:

- How does this child respond to being in a cross-cultural situation?
- What is this child's response to languages other than her own?

Exploring your personal attitudes toward each family and its culture is important. With an affirming attitude, support for the family and home culture becomes a protective factor for the child's identity and family preservation. When reflecting on your feelings about cultural differences, consider these questions:

- What are your attitudes toward diversity and preserving cultural differences? Why do you think you have this attitude?
- Where do your cultural roots lie and how do you feel about them?
- How do you identify yourself culturally today?

- What's the first thing that comes to your mind when you think about the word *culture*?
- What language did your ancestors speak? Do you speak that language? If not, why not?

Looking at Gender and Age Differences

Think about cultural issues around gender. What are differing views on gender roles? What are your views on gender roles? For example, on the one hand there is the perspective that children should be raised androgynously; that is, that they should learn roles that can be adopted by both males and females. This perspective gives priority to equity issues and has the goal of freeing males and females to move beyond the restrictions placed on them for specific expressions of masculinity and femininity. Another perspective rejects the idea of androgyny and values differences between males and females while also looking for paths to equity. Yet another perspective sees strong expectations about how males and females should be and act. The goal is sharply defined gender roles and all adults are expected to teach children what those are. Cultural ideas about gender roles may influence what the family considers appropriate play; they may influence your ideas about who should play what. Maybe even your own gender influences *your* ideas about what's acceptable play and what isn't.

Cultural expectations about age may also impact role definition. Expectations about what a child can do at a particular age are cultural to a large extent. Although the milestones of say, physical development, for example, seem to be universal, culture has an influence even there. (See the next section, Development, for further explanation.) How children are expected to relate to people of different ages is also cultural. For example, in some cultures children out of infancy may be expected to take care of those younger than themselves. They may also be expected to show deep respect for those older than themselves, especially those considered elders.

Implications for Practice

What you know about each family's culture should guide your practice by making you responsive to differences. Remember that we aren't suggesting that you ignore what you know as a practitioner even if it conflicts with what parents believe about or want for their children. We're not suggesting setting aside standards. We are asking you to look closely at where your own limited perspective might be getting in the way of understanding family differences. We are asking that you have discussions about how to incorporate what the parents want and figure out together with the parents how you can respond without them giving up their values or you giving up your professionalism. You can't decide how to handle the issues around children's identity development without consulting with parents. Cultural differences demand a true partnership, not just lip service, if you are to integrate knowledge and practice.

When thinking about approaches to guidance and discipline, consider cultural differences. Diversity in discipline approaches is a big subject and one that has not been extensively studied. We don't expect you to know all about the subject. We are only asking you to be aware that part of your job is to understand what behaviors parents in your program see a need to change and how they go about changing them.

DEVELOPMENT

Although D is for *development*, we also include *learning*, because you can't have one without the other. Learning means changes in behavior as a result of experience. The word *development* comes from Latin and literally means "the unfolding." It's a beautiful image to think of a child unfolding like a rose bud into a rose, and there's some value in it, but it's not completely accurate. Children are not plants; it's not enough to just feed and water them while you sit back and wait for them to grow. Yes, children develop, but they also learn. Both development and learning involve increasingly greater complexity and changes of behavior as children engage with and make meaning of their world.

Appreciating the uniqueness of each individual is an important goal for early childhood educators. At the same time they can look to the science of child development to discover what researchers have laid out in terms of patterns and timelines. Comparisons may be important if a child deviates too far from the charts, but they can also be dangerous when adult expectations put pressures and constraints on children. Here we want to point out the importance of looking at the unique patterns of individual development. Each child is different. Also, the child always comes in a context and this context influences development. For example, when a child belongs to a group that is a target for bias, a good deal of energy goes into reacting to the negative messages and energy that may tie up certain aspects of development (Derman-Sparks, 1989).

Another example of the influence of context on development relates to cultural differences. Say, for instance, that a family puts a high priority on helping the child see him- or herself as first and foremost a member of the group and continually downplays individuality. (See the Home section for an expanded explanation.) In that case, the behaviors of a 2-year-old striving for autonomy or a 4-year-old showing initiative may not be understood in the same way as in a family where individuality is a priority. Practitioners must see how priorities affect perceptions and be willing to accept that some perspectives are different from their own or what they learned in their studies.

Is this child normal? That question may be on the minds of practitioners and parents, but before trying to answer it, it's important to think about what the word *normal* means. Normal has to do with norms, and although those have been established and are continuing to be established, you must always ask who established the norms, when, and why? What population was studied and how was it studied? How is that population similar to or different from the child you are considering? Consider that normal behavior, ability, and developmental progression are all influenced by the context, including the setting or situation, cultural expectations, and the individual priorities and expectations of the people in charge. Comparing, ranking, and rating people is a cultural need and is not universal. In some cultures, comparisons are never made and children are treated as unique individuals.

When trying to understand a child who does not fit typical learning or developmental patterns, it is vital to resist taking a negative view by focusing on what the child can't do. One of the authors was a parent in an infant program designed for children at risk for, or identified with, special needs. Over the diaper changing table was a chart of normal development and it was almost impossible not to notice how the babies being changed didn't fit the chart. The point is to concentrate on what the child *can* do and work from there to help the child move into new territories while expanding present abilities.

Knowing if parents have the same ideas about development as the practitioners is important. We have to be careful about trying to convert everyone to one view instead of listening to and learning from families about their different views. That doesn't preclude practitioners continually taking a close look at where each child stands in regard to developmental milestones. Developmental information can influence interactions but should not negatively affect the image the adult holds of the child. Observation (and perhaps note taking) helps practitioners make decisions about what might help individual children as well as a group of children expand and practice the skills they have in each of the areas of development (physical, intellectual, and social/emotional). Of course, gently encouraging each child to try new things is important too. An experienced practitioner who takes time to look carefully can often see what will probably be next and gently encourage the child in that direction.

Thinking of development as a sand pile instead of a set of stairs helps us find appropriate ways to promote it. The stair-step model is constructed on the idea that particular sets of foundational skills are necessary before the next step is attained. One thing depends completely on another. Programmed learning is built on such a model. We're taking a sand pile view instead. We know that the grains on the bottom support those on the top, but we can't pick out single grains and show how any particular one is essential support for the ones above it.

Complexity is the key to understanding development and learning. The simpler we make it, the more disservice we do to the child and the family. After all that discussion we came up with just three things you need to know about a particular child's development. We are assuming that you either have knowledge about developmental sequences or can find resources to help you ask the questions we've set up for you. Think about a boy who is 3 years old and ask:

- What is he doing developmentally and how does or doesn't he fit the pattern or expectations for his age?
- What is unique about this child's developmental progression?
- How does the family see the child and understand this age group? (It may be different from the way you see and understand it.)

Think about your own ideas and experience with the developmental approach to understanding children. Ask yourself:

- Would you say you are a developmentalist or have developmentalistic tendencies? Or, do you look through a completely different lens to understand how children grow and learn?

Looking at Gender and Age Differences

Now think about a girl and answer the questions again. Then go through each developmental period, asking the questions about both boys and girls. Continue until you have considered all the boys and girls in the age range of birth to 5 years or the age range in your group. Do you consider gender differences when making developmental assessments or do you disregard gender? If you consider gender, are your perceptions and considerations made on particular knowledge you have, your own experience, your own ideas about gender roles and appropriate behaviors, or a combination of the three? Reflect on whether you have different expectations for boys and girls and, if you do, why that might be. Does bias play a part in the way you regard boys and girls? Remember these questions don't have right answers. We're not testing you. We're asking you to pay attention to what you see and judge. We're asking you to look inside yourself. Further, we're asking you to integrate knowledge and practice.

Implications for Practice

What you know about where each child is in his or her developmental progression helps you plan environments, experiences, and opportunities for growth for that child and for the group. What you plan has to be sufficiently open-ended to enable all children to find something in those experiences and take advantage of opportunities, no matter where they are developmentally.

Knowing about development also gives you a basis for talking with parents and finding out if they see things the way you do. When you do that, you learn about varying perspectives, and the ones that don't match yours may affect your decisions about practice.

Developmental considerations also enter into discipline and guidance approaches. What works for an older child doesn't necessarily work for a younger one. Give all children reasons for what you do to guide their behavior, but don't expect the younger children to understand them. Also, don't reason on and on and don't get into arguments.

No child fits the developmental charts perfectly and some don't fit them at all. Don't let ideas of "normal" and "not normal" influence your ability to relate to each and every child and family. Take children as they come.

EMPOWERMENT

Development and learning are not passive processes; children are actively involved in their own growth. We can think of that involvement as one kind of power. Children need the support of adults to validate that power, increase it, and help them learn to use it constructively. We are calling the support adults provide *empowerment*. We don't consider empowerment as giving power to children, but rather recognizing and acknowledging the power each already has. We do that when we trust in each child's own momentum, timetable, interests, priorities, and initiative; when we offer new opportunities to engage with the world; and when we present challenges at appropriate times.

Power is a word with different meanings. If you look to the Latin root of the word, which means "to be able," you can see that one facet of power is ability. You want to know about each child: what are the abilities he or she already has, which ones can be improved on, and what ones does he or she still need to acquire. Some abilities unfold naturally (like learning to walk) but others need adult help, support, or teaching, so we see engaging children in a teaching/learning process as a form of empowerment. Here are some questions to ask about a particular child related to empowerment. Think of a 5-year-old girl:

- Which of this child's abilities are developing without needing more than an environment to develop in?
- Which of this child's abilities need adult support/help and perhaps teaching?
- Which abilities are most important to the child?
- Which abilities is the child focusing on?
- If the child belongs to a group, which abilities are most important to that group?
- Which abilities are most important to the family?
- Which abilities are most important to the community?
- Which abilities are most important to you?

Another facet of power has to do with identity. We are also using the word *empowerment* to mean tapping into what some people call personal power; that is, the ability to be who you really are. That facet brings us to self-esteem. Self-esteem is an assessment of self-worth, and the goal for healthy development is high self-esteem. Children with high self-esteem like themselves. The definition of *self-esteem* includes a realistic assessment. In other words, children with high self-esteem are not oblivious to their weaknesses, but rather they are able to look honestly at themselves and decide that they have more pluses than minuses. Some questions to ask are:

- Does this child have a sense of self-worth? If yes, how does she show it?
- How does the family feel about the child's ways of showing self-esteem? Are they comfortable with them?

The idea of self-esteem and its importance is cultural and fits best in a culture where the emphasis is on individuality. Children whose families have a more collectivist orientation may be taught to be humble. Pride in personal accomplishments may be frowned upon, so it is important not to judge each child's sense of self-worth by the same measuring stick.

A further definition of the self-knowledge aspect of the word *empowerment* comes from Intisar Shareef (1997), a teacher educator and early childhood professional from northern California, who says, "Power is the ability to be who you really are and have other people accept it." She says that, as an African American, this kind of power is particularly important. Her people have had a hard struggle for a long time to define themselves in ways different from the stereotypical ways they are defined by others, including members of the dominant culture in the United States, and especially the media.

What we are pointing out is that all children don't take the same path toward identity development, and it is important for practitioners to understand that. Knowing what support each child needs in his or her identity development is an important part of empowerment. Also, knowing how to help children get beyond stereotypes and deal with biases is part of helping each to form a strong and healthy identity.

The most obvious facet of power is control. We didn't put it first because we wanted you to get a broader view of power. If you think of power as control, which includes self-regulation, that definition brings up a different set of questions to ask about each child. Still thinking about that 5-year-old girl, ask:

- How much does this individual child need help to use power in appropriate ways?
- What are the likely times and situations this particular child will need help to curb, divert, or channel energy?
- What kind of guidance approaches work best with this child?

Looking at Gender and Age Differences

Now we want you to change the girl to a boy and go through the questions again. How are empowerment issues different for males and females? Do girls need more support for empowerment than boys? How aware are you of the existence of sexism in the people and institutions around you? Are you influenced by the stereotypes of the strong male and weak female, or the female who shows emotions and the male who doesn't? Having those stereotypes in mind can help you go deeper when you think about gender differences in this section, especially when you change gender and go through the questions again. When you have asked the questions about a 5-year-old boy, go on to think of an infant girl and see how that changes things. What about a toddler boy? If you work with children, go on to consider all children in the age range in your group. If you haven't thought about a child with a particular physical or developmental challenge, do so, and then go through the questions one more time to discover what is the same or different about empowerment when special conditions exist.

Implications for Practice

One aspect of empowerment is helping children understand limits and learn the benefits of behaving in cooperative ways. Some strategies adults use in guiding behavior are more empowering than others. Here are five strategies that empower:

- Be clear about what you expect and communicate it to the child: "I won't let you run in the street."
- Offer choices. Give two yeses for every no: "You can't run inside, because there's not enough room, but we can go outside and you can run as much as you want. Or maybe you'd like for us to look at a book together."
- Give reasons for your limits: "You can't go into the street by yourself. The street is dangerous. You can get hit by a car."
- Reflect the child's feelings: "I see how upset you are right now."
- Give feedback about your personal feelings: "I felt really scared when I thought you were going to run away from me."

FEARS

All children have fears at one time or another. Some of those fears may seem mysterious or unfounded to us, but are real to them. A toddler, for example, may be afraid of being flushed down the toilet or sucked into the bathtub drain. It's important for adults to know about children's fears, deal with them respectfully, and help children come to terms with them. What children fear depends to some extent on their age, individuality, and experience. Some fears cross age boundaries. Fear of abandonment, for example, is a built-in fear that relates to survival. It shows up in the clinging and crying when parents prepare to leave the child. Sometimes feelings of fear and loss from separation are extreme. Although there are some common patterns of separation behaviors, no two children are exactly alike in the degree of distress, their actual behavior, and their learning of coping skills.

Some common fears in the youngest children are strangers, animals, masks, and lightning. Fearing loud noises is common, too: noises such as thunder and vacuum cleaners. Some children fear the dark. Cognitive development must be considered when trying to understand children's fears. For example, children who don't have language to explain what they are afraid of leave the problem of figuring it out in the hands of the adult. Children too young to understand how things change and what remains the same in spite of change may show fear at seeing the unexpected. They don't realize that Dad is still Dad with his beard shaved or that boys remain boys no matter what their hair looks like or what clothes they wear. Sometimes fears show up as bad dreams, which are the result of the active imagination that children develop by about 2 years of age. Children old enough to both talk and have imaginations can tell you about their fear of monsters and ghosts.

Children who live with violence and crises in their lives or even in the media are likely to have additional worries about their safety and that of their loved ones. Practitioners may find figuring out how to deal constructively with them a challenge because, while they are part of the child's daily life, they may be outside the practitioner's realm of experience. The impact of these fears may cause children to be timid and withdrawn, or the opposite, aggressive and destructive to themselves or to others. These children need comfort, reassurance, and opportunities to feel safe and secure.

Knowing about fearfulness in general is useful, but even more important is knowing what fears each particular child in your service has. Think of an 18-month-old boy and ask yourself:

* How does this particular child show fears?
* How easy is it for you to understand what the child is feeling and what is causing the feeling?
* If the child has language, does he express fear directly through words? Do facial expressions and body language match the words?
* What does he typically do when afraid? What behaviors show up as a typical response to fear?

A common response is to leave the fearful situation by turning away, crawling, or, if old enough, by running. The child may move toward an adult or older child for protection. If the child is quite young or the situation isn't too scary, the child may merely look to someone familiar for reassurance. Sometimes children faced with a fearful situation meet it head-on and fight it. Ask:

* How aware am I of the circumstances that cause this particular child to show fear?
* Where do the fears I've seen in this child come from?

Sometimes children show anger when they feel afraid. Becoming angry gives energy to confront what causes fear. In the face of anger, ask:

- Is fear behind this child's feelings and/or actions?

Fears come from many sources. Some, like fear of falling, are built in from birth and are designed to keep the baby (and the species) alive. Some fears are learned. When Julie plays with a cat that scratches her, she may then fear all cats because of her bad experience. A clown who comes too close, makes faces, and talks too loud may have the same effect. Knowing where a fear comes from helps you know what to do about it. Learned fears can be unlearned. Some fears aren't learned but are part of some children's natural make-up.

Temperament makes a difference. Some children are often fearful of anything new. They are continually cautious and hold back in situations that another child would find exciting, interesting, or fun.

Some fears relate to the priorities of the child's family. Those priorities may or may not be cultural. For example, fear of failure can show up in children where the family emphasis is on successful performance. Fear of being singled out can be a concern of children whose cultural or family imperative is that they should blend in.

To understand each child's fears, the practitioner needs the help of the family. Sharing information is vital. Notice that the theme of sharing information in order to co-construct a picture of the child is woven throughout this book.

To deal with a child's fears, it helps to be aware of your own. Think about:

- What are you afraid of?
- How do you show your fear?
- What do you normally do when you are afraid?
- How can you use your own experience with fear to help children with theirs?

Looking at Gender and Age Differences

When thinking of fear in relation to gender, we suspect we triggered some stereotypes. To discover to what extent, go through and ask the questions again, changing the boy to a girl. Consider how much difference it makes if you are dealing with the fears of a boy instead of a girl. Try thinking about a boy and a girl in different age groups and see if age makes a difference when considering gender. If you are working in an

ECE program, think about each child in your group. Reflect on whether you have different expectations of courage and risk taking for boys and girls. Do your expectations relate to age or do you expect the same from all children? What do families believe about their boys' fears and their ability to face them as compared to their girls'?

Implications for Practice

A safe environment and supportive trusted adults help children deal with their feelings. Support children who are protesting when their parents leave. Be reassuring while at the same time acknowledging their fear and distress. Let them know that they are safe and in good hands. Responding in a warm matter-of-fact way helps children build confidence that they are not abandoned. Having something interesting set up in the environment to attract their attention when they first arrive helps them begin to get involved and feel at home even without their parents. Sometimes children who are upset prefer to get interested in objects, materials, toys, equipment, or activities, rather than being involved with a person. In that case, stay close, but don't force yourself on a child. Having an object from home helps comfort some children. Other children may attach to an object in the program and find comfort in it. Your job is to help children learn all these kinds of coping skills. The skills that help us deal with feelings around letting go of those we love can last a lifetime.

Prevent fearful situations when possible and, when not possible, offer comfort and a variety of opportunities to feel secure. Protect children from hurting each other. Both the child who does the hurting and the victim need protection, as either role is likely to be frightening for a child. We don't always think of children who hurt others as needing protection, but they do. They need to feel secure that someone will help them control their impulses and keep them from hurting others. You can even say something like "I won't let you hurt anybody. I see you need my help to control yourself until you can do it without my help."

Understanding the source of a fear is the first step toward doing something about it. Some fears are learned. The child with a number of uncomfortable experiences with doctors and hospitals may fear white-coated people. If the child learned the fear, careful steps can be taken to help him or her unlearn it by modeling and by exposing the child in small doses in a safe situation with calming, supportive adults. Understanding temperamental differences helps practitioners predict which child needs protection from what kinds of situations, objects, and people. Giving fearful children a strong base of security in the face of new situations can help them. Being patient with naturally cautious children allows them to outgrow some of their fears gradually, although caution may be a lifelong characteristic of some people.

Recognize that fear is often behind anger. For example, children may be angry if they have had unstable lives, whether in multiple foster care placements or in situations where they witnessed or experienced violence. They may take out their anger on people who had nothing to do with the experiences. Instead of returning the anger, be understanding and provide gentle but firm guidance. Angry children need to know that someone is in charge and won't let them get out of control and behave in destructive ways.

GROUP BEHAVIOR

The people we are with affect our behavior. In groups, our behavior is likely to be different from our behavior when we are alone or with one other person. The same is true of children. In general, the older children are the better they are at coping with being in a group. Yet, if you think about it, there are big differences even among adults in how much they enjoy being in groups, how comfortable they are, and how they behave. Picture a party—some adults will be in the thick of things, gregarious, outgoing, moving around, introducing themselves to anyone they don't know, being great conversationalists, appearing to be the life of the party, and having a great time. But that's not everybody. Others talk to a few people rather than circulating; still others stand back and wait to be approached; and a few look distinctly uncomfortable, as though they'd rather be anywhere else than at the party. Some people start off looking uncomfortable and shy, but gradually warm up to the situation. That's how it is with young children.

Temperament, style, preference, and experience all affect how children respond to groups, even children of the same age. Culture and family traditions enter in here too. Some children are always in groups from infancy on, as parents include them in all family activities, including parties as well as religious services. Other children never go to parties or services and are seldom exposed to groups, especially when they are babies.

Of course, being in an early childhood program isn't the same thing as going to a party. In those situations you don't have to concentrate on resting or sleeping, coping with being in a group day after day, or figuring something out. In fact, all you have to concentrate on is being where you are. However, the differences in the adults at a party are in some ways similar to differences in children in ECE programs. In programs, some children, including babies, will be much better than others at tuning out distractions and concentrating on what they are doing, while others will be constantly interrupting their eating, resting, or play to pay attention to what is going on around them. We probably all know some children (and even adults!) who can fall asleep anywhere. You can picture an older baby concentrating so hard on trying to stack three blocks on top of each other that she is oblivious to what is happening around her. Some children become distressed because of too much stimulation from people, sounds, and the physical environment—not very different from the way we might feel after trying to shop in a busy shopping center! Some people who know toddlers very well believe that one common cause of temper tantrums is being where there is too much going on. In other words, sometimes a temper tantrum is a toddler's way of saying "Too much—stop the world, I want to get off."

Another dimension of group behavior is that most groups, whether children or adults, or a mixture of both, have leaders and followers. Of course, these roles may alter in any group according to the situation, but in the early childhood years there is evidence of leadership across a variety of situations in some children. Children who are very social and outgoing often attract the attention of other children, who may follow them. A related phenomenon that many practitioners become very aware of is that, in groups, one child's behavior or mood is likely to affect that of others. If one baby cries, others are likely to start crying. If one toddler starts hitting the table with her hands while waiting for lunch, many toddlers follow. If one 3-year-old starts running around in circles imitating ambulance sirens, others join in. This isn't so much about leadership as it is about herding, or "running in packs," which is typical in groups of young children.

As we wrote previously, some children seem much more influenced by other children, while others characteristically seem to go about their business with less regard to what is going on around them. This makes us think about the power of imitation and modeling. Children learn a lot from adults, but they learn so much from their peers by observing and listening to them. They learn language, skills, knowledge, and ways of doing things and behaving from children their own age as well as younger and older children. Children who come to ECE programs will have varying amounts of experience being with other children. Anyone who has worked for a number of years in ECE programs will vouch for the fact that groups have a particular character that probably comes from many children adopting the ways of being and behaving of a few leaders in the group.

Another type of group behavior happens in ECE programs when children are brought together for an activity, for group time, for eating—times when children are all being encouraged or required to do the same thing at the same time. Of course, this happens more and is more appropriate for children over 3 years than for those under 3 years, but even among older preschool-aged children there will be differences in how readily they participate as a part of a group and how long they can sustain doing something that they have not chosen. Willingness and ability to conform vary in children of the same age. Some children are happy to conform, while others resist more or can cope with not doing their own thing only for a time. Culture enters in here too. When conformity is valued highly, children can perform what seem like amazing feats to those who believe that children cannot sit still for more than a few minutes. In a family where religious rituals include everybody no matter how young, even toddlers can sit for hours. We're not saying you *should* keep young children sitting for hours in a children's program, we're only pointing out that the expectations for conformity vary from culture to culture.

So, to explore how group behavior is different for each child, start by thinking about a girl who is 3 years old and ask these questions:

- What evidence do I have about this child's style of being in a group? Is she a "life-of-the-party" person, one who copes well, or someone who has difficulty coping with the group situation?
- Is there a difference in behavior in a large group and a small group?
- Is this child behaving mostly like a leader or a follower, or does she move back and forth between the two roles equally?
- How does this child cope in our group situation? What are the times that are difficult for her?
- How much does this child seem to be in tune with the group?
- How much does she seem able to tune out distractions when in a large group?
- What experience has this child had in the past and what ongoing opportunities does she have to spend time with other children, older and younger, as well as children her own age?
- What strategies does she use to enter group play?
- How do the parents feel about their child being in a group? Do they have concerns? Do they see being in a group as a positive thing?
- Do they have a preference for a large group or a small group?

You may want to ask yourself:

- What is my own personal style in groups? How does that affect my ideas about working with a group of children?
- Do I prefer large groups, small groups, or being on my own with maybe one other person?

- Do I have ideas about the ideal child in relation to group behavior? Am I sufficiently accepting of different styles, at the same time giving each child support to function well in the group?

Looking at Gender and Age Differences

Does it matter whether it is a boy or a girl when looking at group behavior? Do you have different expectations for boys and for girls? If yes, where did you get these expectations? How about age? Do you expect more of an older child and less of a younger child as far as group behavior? Try going through the questions again, changing age and alternating gender. See what you discover. Did you also consider a child with physical or developmental challenges? How might those particular challenges affect the ability to get along in a group?

Implications for Practice

Consider the overall amount of stimulation in the environment. Of course the need for and tolerance of stimulation varies with temperament and mood, age, time of day, and how tired or rested the child is. In any given group, some children typically need more stimulation and others need less. One way to respond to their varying needs is to create quiet secluded areas so children can withdraw safely and protect themselves from being overstimulated. These areas also provide privacy for those who seek it. Of course, these small, quieter areas must be set up so that supervision is possible. Because of their height, it's possible to make barriers that are tall enough to shield children from each other, but short enough for adults to see over.

When children who are overstimulated have tantrums, taking them away from the stimulation may help. We're not talking about time-out as a punishment, but rather as a chance for the child to calm down and get back into control. Then, when the tantrum is over, think of ways for the child to either stay in a less stimulating situation, or help the child learn to retreat when needed to prevent further frustration resulting in tantrums. Ideally, over time, children come to know themselves sufficiently well that they will "self-administer" time-out when they need it.

Recognize and become skilled at handling what's called *behavior contagion*, which occurs when one or two children start something and the rest join in. You can see this in groups of infants when one starts crying, and that sets the others off. In this case, the spread of the behavior seems to come from an empathic response or a reaction to an unpleasant sound, but behavior contagion also takes the form of games. For example, one child chases another, and soon the whole group has joined them. Or one child screams and the others join. Sometimes, in order to handle this behavior, you have to join in to calm it down. For example, when the noise level of children talking and laughing reached a peak during one group time, one practitioner we know stopped trying to fight it. Instead she announced loudly, "Let's see how loud we can be," and started shouting herself. A chorus of shouts and screams resulted. When the children began to pause for breath she suggested in a loud voice that quickly diminished into a whisper, "Now let's see how quiet we can be, like little mice." It worked. The children started making squeaks and whispering in tiny voices.

Consider focusing some planning time on arranging for small groups of children to spend time together. What are the implications for arranging the environment? How do the small groups gather? What keeps them together? How long do they stay together? How can practitioners support children's relationships in small groups? What is the adult's role when children are in small groups? Where do infants fit in?

Children with physical or other kinds of challenges may need extra help to feel part of a group like everyone else. Before they arrive, environmental accommodations may need to be considered. For example, if the only way to the outside play area involves going down stairs, children in wheelchairs may be excluded from the group at times. Ways need to be found to include children with limited mobility in movement or dance experiences. In addition to environmental considerations, you have to teach children about circumstances they may not have experienced themselves. For example, children with limited hearing may miss conversations that are held behind their backs, so the other children need to know to talk face-to-face with them.

True inclusion in groups is not about making special arrangements or variations to normal provisions to suit children with developmental challenges, but rather ensuring that the provisions for all children work for everyone. There is an important distinction between those two options, and if you think about it, the former isn't really inclusion.

HOME

All children, of course, have a life outside of the ECE program. What kind of life does each have? That the child arrives in a family context, even if you aren't very familiar with that context, is something to keep in mind always. You may not find out much about the family until you get to know each other, and some families you may never know well. Some families are naturally private and others have learned to mistrust people outside the family. Others want to share a lot of information. We're not suggesting you pry or ask a lot of probing questions, especially at the beginning of their participation. We are suggesting that it is always important to keep in mind that children belong to their family, and supporting that family and keeping strong the child's connections with it are primary parts of a practitioner's job.

Below are some questions that may or may not be important for you to have answers to. Some answers may arrive without your having to ask, as the information may come voluntarily from the family. Still others you will figure out over time without asking. When you ask directly about something that seems important but may not be essential for you to know, you run the risk of the family thinking you are prying. Of course, all the information you have about the family must be confidential unless the family gives you permission to treat it otherwise. Discussing one family with another is unprofessional and can create serious mistrust.

It is important for you to know eventually:

- Who lives with the child?
- What is the child's role and place in the family? You can interpret the question any way you like, but we had in mind some of the following questions: Is the child an only child? If not, where is the child in the birth order? What about the gender of siblings? Is the child the only or first grandchild, or the only or first grandchild of that gender? How do parents and other family members view this child; for example, was he planned? Was he born after the death of another child in the family? Is he a stepchild? Is he seen as a peacemaker? Is he seen as a troublemaker? (Obviously, some of these are factual questions that can be asked; others are important things to know, but will become known only indirectly through establishing good communication and a trusting relationship with the family.)
- Who in the family has a close relationship with and/or an influence on the child (whether they live with the child or not)?
- Are there family elders, and what is their role in the family and in relation to the child?
- What language (or languages) is spoken in the home?
- What language (or languages) does the family want the child to speak?
- Is religion a major influence in the home? Will that influence the child's participation in the ECE program? If so, how?
- What cultural influences might impact the child's participation?

- What are the stresses the family deals with?
- What are their strengths for addressing those stresses?
- What kind of environment does this child live in?

Some pitfalls arise around these questions. One such pitfall is the practitioner's own prejudices. For example, if you discover the family has little money and few material possessions, do you immediately label them a "needy family," decide they must be unhappy, and feel pity for them? Do you think of a single-parent family as a "broken home"? Take time to reflect on what assumptions, biases, and prejudices you have about a particular family or families in your program. Then reflect on the positive aspects of the family or families. It's important to look at the strengths each family has. It is also important to realize that each family has skills and knowledge, even if they are very different from those that you have.

Sometimes professionals find the family's ideas out of synch with what they consider good practice. For example, a mother may spoon-feed her 4-year-old and be toilet training her 8-month-old. We've said that it is important to honor diversity and be sensitive to cultural and family differences, so we want to try to explain why families may take such a different approach from professionals.

Families can sometimes be placed on a continuum that has individualists at one end and collectivists at the other. Individualists have independence as a number-one priority, while collectivists see an emphasis on independence and individuality as a threat to their collectivism. A family's orientation to these two ways of perceiving their job as child rearers can drastically affect their ideas of what's best for children. Their ideas shape their expectations when they enter an ECE program. Without understanding the differences, the practitioner and the family can experience serious tensions that may be hard to talk about, especially if either is perceived by the other as having more power.

Training in early childhood education almost always comes more from the individualist end of the continuum. Most professionals have little problem understanding the families who stress independence and perceive their child as an individual. That particular perception influences the way they relate to that child and affects every aspect of their behavior. They may see dependence as a negative thing and do all they can to move the child toward independence. They teach their children that to be grown up is to become an independent individual. They start working toward this goal when the child is an infant. When parents provide a separate bedroom for the baby, that's a clue that they value independence. Teaching self-help skills to babies, toddlers, and preschoolers is another clue.

Of course, just because they stress independence doesn't mean they want their child to be a loner. They are likely to believe that relationships are important too, but the older the child gets the more the independence and individuality of the person become viewed as prerequisites for serious and lasting relationships. In fact, the mark of the ultimate adult relationship is the coming together of two individuals who are secure in their independence. If individuals don't have a sense of self they tend to derive their security from the other, which can give them the label "codependent," which is seen as unhealthy.

In the other group are the collectivist families who stress interdependence and teach their children that they are members of the group first and individuals after that. The role of the individual is to serve the group. Collectivist families perceive their infants as having a strong streak of independence that must be tamed as they are brought into the group. The family's job is to be sure that the tendency toward independence doesn't separate their children from their family and from their people. Sleeping arrangements may be part of that goal, and co-sleeping is often practiced. Instead of teaching self-help skills, adults teach that being taken care of is right, proper, and makes others feel good. Dependence and interdependence are viewed as worthy goals. They also teach, perhaps mostly through modeling, that taking care of others is a better approach than taking care of oneself. Children are urged to care for those younger than themselves. Everyone takes responsibility for caring for the elderly, and caring for someone is considered a privilege, not a burden.

Both of these systems, the individualistic and the collectivistic, provide for needs being met, but in different ways. The first group sees self-care as the ultimate, while the second group sees caring for others as preferable to caring for oneself. The goal is that everybody's needs get met. The first group is still figuring out the means of caring for those who can't care for themselves and is in a conflict about whether the family is responsible or whether the greater society should do it. That last statement shows two things to keep in mind: first, that culture is always changing because to survive people must adapt; and, second, that even independence-minded people realize that people need to take care of those who can't take care of themselves. As stated previously, these two orientations can't be taken as an either-or mind-set. They must be viewed on a continuum. No family wants to rear children to be hermits and no family wants their children to remain so dependent that they are helpless. Both want independent individuals who relate to others. The relative emphasis on one or the other in child rearing is what is different.

In many other parts of this alphabet section, questions and issues related to these two very different perspectives arise. The theme of contrasting individualism with collectivism is embedded throughout the book as one part of the broader discussion of diversity issues.

Some questions to ask in relation to discovering how the family's priorities fit with your own, and those of the program, are:

- What are the indications that the family is more or less independence-minded than you?
- Think about tensions that arise between you and families over ways to do things. Can they be related to the theme of individualism/collectivism?
- How do the skills you want to stress fit with the skills the family wants their child to gain? Do they fit with the family's priorities for their child?
- How important are self-help skills to you? Is your situation such that children can be encouraged to help each other?
- How aware are you of conflicts that can arise with families because of licensing regulations, professional standards, or what are considered best practices?

Looking at Gender and Age Differences

As discussed before in the section called Culture, both gender and age expectations vary from culture to culture. Here we will examine them in light of the information about the difference between a strongly individualistic family and one that is strongly collectivistic. Do you have an inclination to see males as fitting more into the individualistic family and females into the collectivistic one? If your answer is yes, why might that be? Can you imagine switching and seeing males as the more collectivistic ones? Or do you see no connection between gender and the individualist/collectivist continuum? Consider how these two constructs might influence considerations related to age. One consideration is the age at which self-help skills are encouraged. The families with more individualistic tendencies may start teaching self-help skills early compared to the collectivistic families, who may never teach them at all. Some collectivists assume that children will eventually just figure out by being around other people how to feed themselves and that the skill doesn't need to be taught. What does need to be taught is to accept help from older, more skilled people.

Implications for Practice

When a child who has specific physical or developmental challenges arrives in a program, the family and the practitioner may disagree about what is needed. One family may push self-help skills more than you think they should. Another family may seem to think that being dependent forever is a blessing to the family and the child and not worry about teaching self-help skills at all. The explanation for these two views may relate to the first family being an individualistic one and the second being collectivistic. Or there may be other explanations. Sometimes within a family there may be disagreement about what the child needs.

Exercise caution about leaping to conclusions about families and labelling them or their children. Don't diagnose people using armchair psychology. Do get to know each family and what they want for their children. Together with the family, co-construct an approach to the care and education of each child that fits both the parents and the program. Yes, it's a big job. It might seem much easier to apply a one-size-fits-all curriculum to everybody, but we hope we have convinced you by now that what we propose is worth the extra effort it may take.

INTERACTIONS

Interactions, relationships, and social skills are related ongoing themes in this book. This particular section focuses on interactions that relate particularly to social skills. All behaviors, including the ones indicating social skills, come both from the child's genetic background and from what the child has learned from experience. In other words, behaviors come from heredity and environment and the interaction between the two. Getting along with others relates to age, personality, and temperament, as well as to what the child has been taught or has picked up from those around him or her. And, of course, there are cultural differences. Culture influences social skills a good deal, so it is important to remember not to measure all children on a single measuring stick when it comes to their socialization.

Babies exhibit social behaviors at birth and by a year old they welcome social interaction at times and reject it at other times. Some babies show more of one behavior than the other. Children with disabilities may not show the behaviors that indicate acceptance of interaction in the same way as typically developing children, and it's important to remember that. A child with cerebral palsy, for example, may push away when meaning to get close. As with all children, the adult must learn to pick up the intent behind the signals the child is sending, even if they aren't the same as the signals another child sends.

Early childhood professionals can influence the environment, so teaching social skills is important and begins in infancy. Much of the teaching can be done by modeling, as most children naturally imitate what they see.

Here are some questions to ask about social skills. Think about a 4-year-old girl. Ask the following questions:

- What evidence can you see that she is on the way to gaining the social skills to get what she needs and/or wants?
- Is she developing skills for engaging other children positively?
- Does she have some ideas and skills about how to enter a group playing together and find acceptance?
- Does she show signs of gaining some understanding about the consequences of her actions on others?
- Does she demonstrate both leader and follower skills?
- Does she have any physical, social, emotional, language, or other developmental differences that make it hard for her to interact?

Think too about style:

- What is this child's social style? Is she gregarious, outgoing, a loner?
- Does she prefer to interact with adults or children, or does she interact appropriately with both?
- What kind of help does she need to expand on her style?

Because all the interactions involved in social skills is such a big subject (many books have been written about socialization), we are going to focus on three categories of interactions that are of special interest to ECE practitioners. They are:

1. sharing;
2. aggression; and
3. problem solving.

Sharing

Sharing is a complex issue and therefore difficult for children to figure out. We share toys, but not our toothbrushes. Do I have to share my favorite teddy bear or special blanket that I always have with me when I'm not at home? Do I share my precious doll that I brought from home for show and tell, even though my mom told me to take good care of it and not let it get lost or broken?

Cultural perspectives on sharing complicate the issues further. Adults' expectations of sharing influence how it is learned. In a culture where personal possessions are the norm, children have to learn about owner-ship before they can truly understand the concept of sharing something. A 2-year-old who holds a toy out of reach of a peer or sibling trying to grab it and says "Mine!" is seen as developing the idea of ownership. It may be annoying, but taking pride in ownership and protecting one's possessions can be a cultural imperative, and sharing may be in con-flict with this imperative. If something precious is shared, it may be lost, damaged, or destroyed. So teaching children to share has complexity that makes it difficult and sometimes controversial. It may be hard to be around children who are in conflict because they are still learning their power to possess, but it is nonetheless regarded as a positive step by many and a necessary prerequisite for eventually sharing possessions.

In a communal or collectivist culture where personal possessions are minimal or nonexistent, sharing is taught from birth and ownership is de-emphasized. Children are always expected to share, just as they are always expected to put other people first. These are important cultural lessons, and in this context sharing doesn't have the same complexity or controversy connected to it. Of course, in cross-cultural settings, children may be caught between two perspectives and everything, including shar-ing, takes on considerable complexity until the adults involved sort out what is best for this child or this group in this situation. Think about a 2-year-old girl and ask the following questions:

- What do the parents want the child to learn about sharing?
- What are my own perspectives on sharing and how do they fit with what this parent and other parents in my program want and believe?
- What am I going to do to deal with differing views if they exist?

Looking at Gender and Age Differences. Do you see gender as a factor in children learning to share? Do you see age as a factor? Are infants and toddlers capable of sharing, in your mind? Do you teach sharing differ-ently to different aged children?

Implications for Practice. It's hard to suggest how to deal with sharing without knowing you and the families you serve. The practice of teach-ing sharing needs to be worked out between you and the families, taking everyone's values into consideration.

Aggression

We can't talk about aggression without mentioning assertiveness. Al-though the two may be confused, we see a big difference between them.

Aggression is behavior that hurts or damages, and assertiveness is behavior that makes an individual's needs known and values clear. In cultures that emphasize independence and individuality, assertiveness is a
valued trait and relates to the idea that everybody has the right to express
themselves as individuals. Two assertive individuals negotiate their differences, and this particular skill is taught to children as soon as they can
walk and talk, or even before.

In collectivist cultures that de-emphasize individuality and stress interdependence, the focus is on the needs and wants of the other person,
so assertiveness is frowned upon. The idea is for each to look out for the
other, so the needs get met, but not by the person who has them. It works,
but it's a different system. A person who goes by one system may misun-
derstand the other system completely. It's easy to judge as inferior something that is not understood.

Aggression is different from assertion, although it may be confused
by those who de-emphasize individuality. Aggressive behavior in young
children includes hitting, biting, grabbing, and even extends to verbal
insults and putdowns. If aggression is defined as behavior intended to
harm, then the term *aggression* doesn't fit a lot of the things that young
children do that cause harm, because often they have no understanding
or only limited understanding of the effects of their actions. Children may
hit or bite or push, but their behavior sometimes isn't intended to have the
impact that it does. Think about an 18-month-old boy and ask the following questions:

- How much does this child engage in behavior that hurts others?
- Does he understand the connection between his actions and the
  response of the other child?
- What is he trying to achieve with his behavior?
- Are anger, frustration, boredom, or experimentation part of the
  reason for the behavior?
- What typically triggers hurtful or destructive behavior in this
  child?
- What is the family's attitude toward aggression and also
  assertion?
- Is there a sex role component to whether the family encourages or
  discourages forceful behavior?
- What are your feelings about aggression and its expression?
- How might your feelings affect your responses to this child's and
  other children's behavior?

Looking at Gender and Age Differences. How much do you think gender is a factor in young children's assertiveness and aggression? Are boys

more aggressive than girls if you take a broad definition of aggression and include subtle and blatant verbal attacks? Do boys tend to be more assertive? If you answered yes to both questions, what role might teaching play in boys being different from girls? Is it possible that adults encourage or even teach aggression and assertion to boys more than to girls? Can girls be taught to be assertive? Do you think it is appropriate for girls to be assertive? For boys?

Certainly age becomes a factor if you compare an infant to a toddler to a 4-year-old. A toddler may lash out, but is likely to be unclear about the impact or real result of his or her behavior. Some aggressive behaviors may have the opposite motive. A bite, for example, may have the same intention as a kiss; that is, a way of expressing love or affection. Similarly, a bite may be more about exploring the texture and substance of another child's arm than the expression of an intention to hurt. Of course, some aggression is intended to hurt. A 5-year-old, for example, may even make a plan to hurt and carry it out.

Implications for Practice. Prevention is more effective than any other approach when dealing with hurtful behavior in young children. Careful attention to each child helps practitioners learn to predict the circumstances under which a hurtful act is likely to happen and enables them to stop it. Some children engage in undesirable behavior because they need more attention than they get, and a kick or a bite brings a dramatic response and an adult over to pay attention to them. In other words, they have figured out that it's the best or only way to get attention from adults. For some children, even a stern negative reaction from an adult is a way of getting the recognition they so desperately seek and is preferable to being ignored.

Most practitioners teach children to use words instead of physical actions to express feelings and assert their rights. Of course, not all parents find this kind of teaching fits into their beliefs about self-expression and the proper way to handle incidents. It's important to talk to families and learn their ideas about what aggression is and how they handle it.

Careful attention to the environment is another approach to dealing with hurtful behavior. Some environments invite chaos and conflict, which can increase undesirable behavior in young children. For example, in a group of toddlers who are all fairly new to the group, having enough toys and duplicates of the most popular ones can cut down on conflict. Of course, this approach fits for people who see objects as important to young children's development and learning. Not all cultures look at toys and materials for toddlers in the same way.

Modeling caring and respectful behavior is another approach. When adults respond to aggression with their own aggression, they model the very behaviors they are trying to diminish. Careful attention to one's own behavior changes that situation.

Problem Solving

Often the answer to undesirable behavior is the use of problem solving skills. Again, this whole subject is more appropriate to cultures that are individualistic and stress independence. Some adults with that orientation are looking for evidence of individual ability to solve problems, starting with infants. The goal is for the child to learn to solve his or her own problems whenever possible, while at the same time recognizing the relative helplessness of infants. Infants use others to help them solve their problems, but the goal of an individualistic practitioner is to get children to become more and more independent in solving their problems. An important aim is to get to the point that when two children have a disagreement over, say, a toy, they can talk to each other, express their feelings, and negotiate a solution without adult assistance.

Parents with a collectivist orientation will probably be far less interested in (and may even distrust) the kind of independent problem solving just described because it doesn't fit their perspective on the relative roles of adults and children. Helping someone younger and less able is more important than two equal peers sorting things out themselves.

Think of a 5-year-old girl and ask:

- What is the family's view of problem solving?

If the goal is independence:

- What evidence can you see of this particular child's growing ability to solve problems when a need or want is frustrated and a conflict occurs?
- Does she use language to work toward solutions that are satisfactory to all involved?

If the child comes from a family that stresses interdependence:

- What evidence can you see of this child's ability to get help to solve problems?
- Does she also show growing skills to help younger children with their problems?

Looking at Gender and Age Differences. Do you see gender as a factor in children learning to problem solve? We hope by now that you are finely tuned to seeing your personal reactions around gender as you go through the many questions with a girl in mind. We hope with each section you continue to consider switching gender and repeating the same questions. That way you can tell if gender makes a difference or not from your perspective.

Obviously age is a factor in problem solving. Infants can't express their problems in words and need help to solve them. Toddlers can solve many of their own problems if that is a value and they are given time and support to do so. By the age of 3, language is becoming a part of problem solving, and by the time children are 4 and 5 years old, they can learn to say what the problem is and even talk their way through solutions.

Implications for Practice. It's hard to suggest how to deal with problem solving without knowing you and the families with whom you work. If you are to support children learning to solve problems, then you have to allow children to have problems. It's hard for adults to step back and let a child struggle to put on a coat or find the right puzzle piece, but if you help too soon the child comes to depend on the help. The trick is to step in at just the moment before the child gives up. Then you provide the least help possible so the child is encouraged to continue to work on the problem. The same is true when two children are in conflict and are trying to straighten it out themselves.

Stepping back is a message about the value of solving problems, but it isn't enough. Problem solving also needs to be taught, including the assertion of needs and rights and the art of negotiation. If you have embraced our message about honoring differences and talking to families when there is a conflict between two perspectives, you are modeling the very approach we are suggesting you teach to children.

JUDGMENT

The concept of judgment takes us into behavioral issues and thinking processes. It also gets into moral issues. Faulty judgment can be a safety issue. Toddlers don't think twice about running out in the street after a ball. They don't understand that the street is dangerous and, even if told, they can't be counted on to remember. Toddlers lack judgment and can't be allowed to go into the street at all because they can't tell the distance of cars or their speed.

Age is, of course, an important consideration. The younger the child, the more likely it is that reasoning will be faulty. Young children don't have the same logic as older ones and adults; in fact it would be accurate to say that all children in the age range that is the focus of this book have faulty logic. They don't understand the more complex workings of cause and effect. A classic example is the child who runs into a light pole on his tricycle. A few days later the electricity goes off all over town, and he thinks he caused it. A sadder and much more serious example is when a child gets angry at her new baby brother and wishes he'd go away. If that baby happens to die, the child blames herself. It's often the case that children blame themselves when parents separate or divorce. Or even sadder is when a child is sexually abused and thinks it was her fault. In these cases, faulty judgment leads to emotional issues and magnifies feelings of shame and guilt.

Certain ways of looking at things, sometimes called habits of thought, can affect children's judgment and therefore their behavior. Children who have used aggression consistently to get their way may see that as the only approach. It's learned behavior because when they hit or grab, they are rewarded by getting what they want. Once they find it works, they don't think; they just impulsively use aggression. This kind of learned behavior bypasses judgment and becomes a knee-jerk response.

Highly aggressive children may also have a tendency to jump to conclusions about motives in others and see hostility where none exists. For example, a child pulling a wagon accidentally bumps into another child. The bumped child immediately jumps on the first child and starts hitting, never considering intention. Even if the child apologizes and says the bump was an accident, the first child doesn't believe it. Faulty judgment at work again. Furthermore, some children may have limited capacity to consider consequences before they act. They may act impulsively and not think things out logically: "Well, if I do that, x is likely to happen." The resulting consequences, such as being hit back or being put in time-out, don't curb the behavior.

In summary, what we are saying about problem solving and aggression is:

- Children learn aggression by being rewarded for it.
- Once learned, judgment isn't used—aggression becomes a knee-jerk response.
- There is a tendency in those who use aggression constantly to discount the intention of the other.
- When this happens, the child isn't thinking about consequences.

It's as though because of habits of thought and the resulting behavior, children suspend judgment to get what they want or relieve their feelings through aggression. Children who don't think about consequences can be surprised by what happens after they start hitting. They may not even make the connection between their action and the subsequent reactions. They not only don't consider consequences, but they also don't see any options other than aggression when faced with a problem.

Think about a 3-year-old boy. Here are some questions to ask about the behavioral aspects of his ability to judge:

- How sensible or realistic is this child's judgment?
- Is he progressing toward understanding cause and effect?
- Does his poor judgment get him in trouble?
- Is he showing evidence of developing problem-solving skills?
- How well does this child understand right and wrong?
- What experience does this child have in caring and being cared for?

And what about you? Here are some self-reflection questions:

- How do you feel about your own ability to make judgments, predict cause and effect, and solve problems?
- Are you a person who has strong feelings about the difference between right and wrong?
- How do you feel about a child's lack of judgment?

Looking at Gender and Age Differences

By now you know our little game of changing age and gender. What happens if you turn the boy into a girl? What happens if you turn them both into a 2-year-old? Does any of this apply to 6-month-olds? Does any of this apply to children who have mental or emotional challenges?

Implications for Practice

Where children lack judgment, it is up to the practitioner to supply it. Furthermore, when children use aggression consistently to get what they want, the practitioner has to interrupt the pattern and teach alternative ways of resolving conflicts (see Interactions). Talking children in conflict through what happened is important if they are to understand each other's motives. Get down on their level and say what you saw happen, or if you didn't see what the conflict was about, say what you are seeing at that moment: "I see you are angry, Josh. Amy, you're crying." Make your tone neutral and leave judgments out of it. Think of yourself as a sportscaster instead of a referee. Make short statements and then be quiet so they can respond. If they begin to explain to you, get them to talk to each other. Helping them understand consequences by making the connection between their behavior and what happened provides a real service to children who don't think before they act. It isn't easy to change things if children are impulsive and don't think about their actions, especially if they have been rewarded by getting attention or their way.

We said in Chapter 1 that we were not going to treat the topic that is usually called discipline as a separate topic, but rather would treat it as one of the many kinds of teaching and learning that happen in an ECE program. One of the aspects of discipline that practitioners are most eager to discuss is setting limits, another area of practice that relates to both adults' and children's judgment. One of the most important things that adults do to support children's learning and development is to set sensible limits that keep them safe and healthy on the one hand and allow them to explore and try things on the other. Deciding what are reasonable limits is sometimes complex and requires adults to exercise judgment. What is reasonable depends on many factors: the child's developmental level, the situation, and the likely risk. The long-term aim in setting limits is for children to come to understand those limits and eventually to have the willpower or self-control to set limits for themselves, which is what self-discipline is all about. When adults help young children take part in the decision-making process about what limits to set and why, children get practice that can eventually lead them to setting their own for themselves.

Children need the security that comes from knowing that sensitive, sensible, and caring adults will set limits for them when children cannot set them for themselves and help them to go along with those limits. Sometimes this is because of their limited understanding and faulty judgment; at other times it is because they lack the willpower or self-control to stay within the limits that they know exist. They also need for limits to be set and enforced in ways that allow them to learn to take care of themselves, others, and the world around them. The younger the child, the less likely he or she is to have self-control and understanding. Therefore, the younger the child, the more likely it is that the adult will have to use actions as well as words to set limits. It would make life easier if we could learn from one experience, but mostly we don't. This means that children learn rules and limits only over time and through repeated experiences.

Adults should set and enforce limits with an attitude of helpfulness rather than being punitive. This attitude allows for firmness but also lets children know the adults are on their side. It is as though the adult is saying through behavior and words, "I know this is hard for you, so I will help you to go along with it."

Too few limits are as ineffective as too many. It is worthwhile for adults working with children to stop and think every now and then about the limits they set and ask themselves the questions: Is this limit necessary? If so, why? Is it for the children's well-being or the adults' convenience? How can I reinforce this limit to make it a constructive learning opportunity for the children?

KNOWLEDGE

We are including mental (or cognitive) skills with knowledge. Knowledge has to do with what is known, while mental skills are the processes for acquiring and using that knowledge. Knowledge is broad enough to include all about how the world and the things in it work, how people behave, and how to do things. We are also including academic skills such as learning to read, write, use numbers, and think mathematically. Academic skills are sometimes the focus of a lot of attention, but we want to point out here that they are only tools. The idea of mental skills goes way beyond those particular tools. Problem solving and making judgments are two mental skills we've talked about that don't necessarily need academic tools.

Babies' mental skills are different from those of toddlers and especially those of 3-, 4-, and 5-year-olds. It may appear to some people that babies aren't thinking but rather just lying around not doing anything much for the first weeks or even months. Wrong! They are busy trying to figure out what they are seeing, hearing, smelling, touching, and tasting. They sort out what is familiar from what is not. They appreciate the familiar as it relates to people and places they know, which gives them a sense of security and builds attachment.

They also seek novelty and are attracted to things that are slightly different from what they know. Children enjoy experiences that are novel enough to be interesting, but not so different as to be scary. Matching the right level of novelty to each baby is the task of the practitioner. As babies begin to move around they use their senses and their muscles to explore and figure things out. Piaget (1952) called this way of acquiring knowledge sensorimotor (*motor* meaning "movement"). So, putting things in the mouth isn't just an unsanitary habit, but rather an important way of acquiring knowledge by using coordination of the muscles, which gets the fingers around the object and the object to the mouth and nose, which brings the tactile senses into play along with the sense of taste and smell.

As children grow older they begin to make what Piaget called mental representations (Evans, 1973), which means they can hold the image of an object, person, or event in their minds. Of course, no one ever saw or measured a mental representation. It's only a construct. But Piaget based his idea on behaviors that indicated the child remembered something from the past. For example, engaging in pretend play depends on the child remembering something seen before, such as using a broom to sweep a floor. The older the child, the greater complexity pretend play takes on. Eventually children can imitate roles, including their perceptions of mothers, fathers, doctors, police officers, even dogs. This is the time that gender roles they've seen and learned about become visible.

Each child and family brings knowledge and life experiences to the early childhood program. For example, a child who has a chronic illness or condition may be an expert on hospitals and doctors. Finding out about families' interests, hobbies, and resources means that the practitioner may be able to find ways to use those to enrich the experience of the children. A child whose family owns a plant nursery may have a lot of experience of gardening. Many children know a lot more about certain subjects than we do.

Early childhood practitioners need to find out at the beginning with each new child about that child's funds of knowledge and mental skills. They also need to know what knowledge and skills are valued by the family. The following questions can help. Consider a 4-year-old girl:

- What is the child interested in knowing?
- What is important for this child to know (given her age)?
- What mental skills does the child have and what ones does the child lack?
- What does the child need to learn next?
- What knowledge and particular mental skills are important to the parents and to the child eventually growing up to fit into the culture of the family?
- What areas of knowledge and kinds of mental skills are important to the community and to the child eventually growing up to function as a community member?
- What areas of knowledge and kinds of mental skills are important to the society and to the child eventually growing up to function as a member of both the greater society and the world beyond it?
- Who, besides the professional asking the questions, can support, guide, and mentor this child in further learning, development, and acquisition of knowledge and mental skills?
- What particular funds of knowledge and mental skills does the child bring personally and from home that she can share with the other children?

- Does this child have any disabilities that affect the way she acquires, processes, and uses knowledge?

Ask yourself:

- How do I feel about my own knowledge?
- Is this an area I feel good about?
- How does the kind of knowledge I have relate to that of the parents in my service?
- Are there some kinds of knowledge I appreciate more than others?

Looking at Gender and Age Differences

If you asked the same questions about a 4-year-old boy, would gender make a difference? Do you believe that there are particular areas of knowledge more appropriate to females and others more appropriate to males? Are you convinced that girls can learn some things easier than boys and vice versa? As already pointed out, age makes a difference in not only the amount of knowledge and the content of the knowledge, but also the way that knowledge is acquired and stored.

Implications for Practice

Good early childhood experiences are about helping children to acquire knowledge and skills in a range of areas. Just as important, or perhaps more important, it is in the early years of life that we want children to gain a passion for learning and a picture of themselves as capable learners. It is often said that one of the benefits of working in ECE programs in contrast to teaching in a school is that usually there is not a prescribed curriculum that dictates the content of the experiences. Early childhood practitioners can focus on what children are doing, what they are interested in, what excites them. Through doing this, children's thinking is extended. In other words, in ECE programs, typically, learning to learn is considered more important than the actual content. In many programs there is pressure to focus on academic or school-related skills and knowledge, most particularly early literacy and numeracy. If these skills are priorities, it is important that they are taught in a way that has meaning for children and responds to what they are interested in rather than being imposed artificially. Providing a print-rich environment and embedding reading, the richness of stories and books, and how and why to use numbers and counting in the experiences of the children is the way to excite them about becoming literate and mathematical.

Using the knowledge, interests, and resources that the child and family bring validates their experience, gives them a sense of belonging through making an important contribution to the group, and broadens the repertoire of experiences available to all children.

Some obvious implications of knowledge are some points we have made many times in this book. All children need a rich environment that provides opportunities to:

- stretch their knowledge and skills;
- consolidate and practice skills and use knowledge already acquired;
- learn from each other by observing as well as working and playing;
- grapple with challenges and solve problems;
- get help from sensitive, wise adults when they need it; and
- experience a balance of the security that sameness and predictability provide and the excitement and challenge of novelty.

LEARNING STYLES

One child, when confronted with a new object or material, always puts it straight to her nose to smell it. This child has an amazing sense of smell. She can pick up an article of clothing, smell it, and identify the person to whom it belongs. Using smell is not a recognized learning style, but we are using this example to show how children use different senses or modalities to understand the world and the things in it.

The more usual learning styles are classified as visual (having to do with the eyes and seeing), auditory (having to do the with ears and hearing), and kinesthetic (having to do with the body; that is, touch and movement). Of course, young children use all three styles to explore and take in information. A 4-year-old finds a snail in the garden and brings it inside. The children gather around to explore the snail. They look at it, listen to the adult talk about it, and touch it. If the adult follows up with experiences, resources, and materials to take the learning further, she may find that some children are drawn to certain types of provisions more than to others. The child who stands around touching it the longest may be a kinesthetic learner—also the one who is out looking for more snails! The kinesthetic learner may also slither around on the floor imitating the snail's movements or instead draw pictures of snails. This child is using the body with its muscles and sense of touch to learn. The child who spends more time looking at the snail and is drawn to books and pictures of snails has the tendencies of a visual learner. The one who asks the adult for more information, wants a story told or read about snails, or listens to tapes with snails as the subject has the tendencies of an aural or auditory learner.

Identifying the child's favored learning style is not of primary importance in the kind of program we've envisioned in this book, where learning is defined broadly and takes place in a rich environment so a child can use multiple senses to explore and understand. The reason we mention it is that some children are drawn to certain kinds of experiences and opportunities that relate to their learning style. Those children running around outside all the time, constantly moving their bodies and never seeming to sit down and focus on visual or auditory experiences, may be kinesthetic learners. They aren't taking time out from learning when their bodies are in motion; rather, they're learning with them.

Think about a 5-year-old boy. Some questions to ask to help find out about this particular child's ways of approaching learning are:

- In what ways and how often does this child use listening skills?
- In what ways and how often does this child use visual approaches to learning?
- In what ways and how often does this child use his body to learn?
- What might the child be learning by moving and touching?
- What are the family's ideas on how children best learn; on how their child best learns?
- Might past experience influence this child's tendency to use eyes, ears, or body more?
- What might be some cultural influences on ideas about individual learning styles and the best ways to learn?
- What physical challenges or developmental differences might affect this child's learning style?

Ask yourself:

- What do I know about my own learning style?
- How does my own learning style affect what I provide for the children I work with?
- How do children's learning styles impact on my feelings about them?

Looking at Gender and Age Differences

What is your experience about how learning styles relate to gender? Does it seem that more boys have one style and more girls have another? What about age? Can you see tendencies toward one style or another in infants? In toddlers? Certainly temperamental differences show up even at birth. Do you think that temperament relates to learning styles?

Implications for Practice

As mentioned before, if a variety of experiences is available for children to choose from, many of them open-ended, then differences in learning styles can be accommodated easily. The kinesthetic learner may be the one who is most misunderstood. The child who has to touch everything even though he is no longer a toddler is taking information in through his fingertips. Adults tend to put more value on the visual and auditory learner, maybe because those styles fit the environment and expectations they will encounter in school, and children with those learning styles are perhaps easier to cater to and work with. Kinesthetic learners can get very frustrated in environments where they can't be active, move around, touch things, and turn what they are learning into activities they can perform with their bodies.

By exchanging information about learning styles with parents, you may find out more about the child as well as the family's ideas about how he or she should be learning. You may also help the family to appreciate their child's individuality. If they already know about learning styles, you can help them see ways to support their child in the future when he or she is in school. For example, knowing that a child needs to hear a word spelled out loud to learn to spell it can be important information later on.

MAJOR LIFE EVENTS

What is a major life event for one person may be relatively insignificant for another. It isn't the event itself, but rather the meaning the person gives to it that makes the difference. There are some events, however, that usually are interpreted as major. Still, we can't assume that an individual's interpretation or reaction to any event is the same as another person's or our own would be. You want to know what major life events each child has experienced, especially if the family perceives that there have been lasting effects. Just as we said about cultural background, however, it's not as simple as just asking the question at the intake interview. Some major life events will be shared only when the family is comfortable with you and there is mutual trust. And some families are more private than others and may never want to tell you certain things.

Just being born is a major life event and affects some children more than others, depending on the circumstances. Even an easy birth is a dramatic event, but most babies get over it quickly. The after-effects of a difficult or early birth can last a long time. If a child is born 3 months early, struggles to live for the next 4 months, undergoing many painful and frightening hospital procedures, and finally goes home with all these experiences behind him, what makes him different from a baby who didn't go through so much? That's something you may want to think about. Has the prematurity affected the parent–child relationship? Perhaps the baby has delicate health and needs to be carefully monitored. He is at risk for Sudden Infant Death Syndrome (SIDS), which means you want specific information on how he needs to be cared for and especially how to position him for sleeping.

Below are some questions about a particular child and her major life events. Remember, by no means are we suggesting that you just go out and ask parents these things. Make this child a 15-month-old girl.

- What major changes has this child experienced recently? In the past?
- Has there been a divorce or separation?
- Has there been a move?
- Has there been a change in the family?

> A sibling born or someone new come to live in the family?
> A parent or other close family member moving out?
> A nanny leaving?
> The death of a parent or other close family member?

- Has violence in the family or community been part of this child's life?
- Has the child experienced a natural disaster?

Those are big events in a child's life, events that have the potential to affect her drastically. Little events can be important too. An event that makes a difference can sometimes be perceived as a happy one, yet may have a negative effect on an individual child. For example, a widow remarries and everyone is happy for her. What meaning does this event have for her 5-year-old? It's hard to know.

Young children may have a hard time expressing what's wrong and what they think or how they feel about it. You have to read their behavior. Ask yourself these kinds of questions, and this time make the child a 4-year-old boy:

- Has there been a change of behavior?
- Does the child seem nervous or anxious?
- Does the child seem unusually sad or subdued?
- Does the child seem especially aggressive?
- Does the child seem unusually frightened or wary?
- Is the child unsettled?
- Does the child end up a victim more often than other children?
- Have the child's normal play themes changed?
- Do you get any clues about what may be troubling the child from his art, music, or movement?
- Does the child seem to be playing out a major life event using toys or other people?

Ask yourself:

- How might major events in my own life affect my reactions to those of a particular child or family? Can I think of examples?
- How might the major events in my life, both long ago and more recently, impact generally on my work with young children and their families?

Looking at Gender and Age Differences

Is there a difference in the ways boys handle major life events and the way girls do? How much difference does age make? If you go back through the questions and think about gender and age you may come up with answers to those questions from your experience.

Implications for Practice

Early care and education professionals are not expected to be psychologists and make diagnoses. At the same time, they may be the first people who are able to step back far enough to see what the family can't see because they are too close to the situation, or are unable to acknowledge what they see. Be careful about jumping to conclusions when you are interpreting children's play and creative expression. The child hitting baby dolls in the doll corner or pretending to cut them up and bake them in the oven is not necessarily a child who has seen or been the victim of violence. She may be just showing a healthy imagination or some frustrated feelings of aggression, or she may be imitating or reacting to something seen on television.

Don't read deep psychological meaning into everything, unless you are fully qualified to do so. For example, one child drew a lovely sunshiny picture and then covered it completely in black crayon using strong strokes. His teacher was worried about depression, but when asked if he wanted to talk about his picture, he explained that it was a day and night picture. First it was day and then it was night and all dark. Nothing deeply psychological there! The same was true when a child brought home only purple paintings for a period of time and the parents thought it was a sign that something was troubling the child. It turned out to be the end of the fiscal year, and that was the only color paint left in the cupboard! Another child was drawing bloody daggers and skulls, but they turned out to be skateboard logos he was copying.

It's sad to think of young children going through unpleasant events that change their lives forever. It's hard to see young children hurting. But this quote from Hemingway (in *A Farewell to Arms*) may give us some comfort: "The world breaks everyone and afterwards many are strong at the broken places."

It's part of the early childhood practitioner's job to help children become strong at the broken places.

NEEDS

One of the messages of this book is about the image of the child the professional holds in mind. We're asking you to maintain an image of a competent and capable child, not a needy, helpless, underdeveloped, or ignorant one. The image adults hold of a child affects the way they treat him or her. Although the needy child image may make us feel useful as early childhood professionals, keeping that image is a disservice to the child and sends messages that do more harm than good. As people whose work has focused on infants and toddlers, both authors have seen how sometimes babies and toddlers are seen as less complex or less clever than preschool-aged children. Sometimes policymakers and bureaucrats look at the preschool years as the time to get children "ready to learn" at school. This phrase—*ready to learn*—gained popularity in the United States in the 1990s and is still being used. Our message is that each child has amazing capabilities that need to be acknowledged and respected. An 18-month-old is not an underdeveloped 3-year-old. A 4-year-old is not an "unready" school beginner.

So we don't want to discuss needy children, but we do want to talk about the concept of needs as valid. We want to look at needs common to all children and special needs related to developmental characteristics and to the individual. We never move beyond basic needs. All of us must have our physical needs met: for air, food, water, rest, warmth, shelter, and elimination. It should be a given that adults in ECE programs are aware of and provide for children's basic needs. We say "should be" because sometimes adults withhold the fulfilment of basic needs for various reasons, including schedules, inadequate numbers of adults for the number of children, groups that are too large, convenience, or to get the child to conform to a group rhythm. We're asking you to think about a particular child in your service and consider how often that child has to wait to have basic needs fulfilled. How often does someone say to this particular child, "You have to wait to rest because it isn't naptime yet" or "I know you are hungry but lunch isn't here yet"?

Now we want you to think of a boy who is a 1-year-old and ask yourself:

- How constant and how urgent are this child's needs?
- Is the child asking for attention because he has a true physical need or because he needs adult attention? (The need for attention is as real as a physical need.)
- What effect does it have on the child to require him to wait?
- How does the child cope with the wait? What are some behaviors you have seen? Do these behaviors work for the child?

We don't mean to imply that children can't learn to delay having their needs met. They can, and they need to eventually learn that they can't always have them met instantaneously. But they don't need extra practice waiting when they are young. In an early childhood program, even when the adults' intention is to meet each child's needs quickly, there will inevitably be times when the child has to wait anyway. We do want to point out that constant delays can have negative consequences. The consequences are the strongest in the first year of life when infants need to learn that they can trust. When needs aren't met in a fairly timely manner, the result is a sense of distrust, according to Erik Erikson (1963).

Another level of physical needs has to do with physical activity. Children need to explore, manipulate, and experience novelty. Think again of a particular child. Make the child a 2-year-old boy:

- How much have you observed or do you know about this child's need for activity?
- Does the child seem to need more activity than the environment allows?

- What does the child do when the circumstances are not right for engaging in physical activity—exploratory and/or manipulative?
- Does the child get frustrated when needs for activity are thwarted? If yes, how does the child cope?

Another level of needs relates to safety. Children have individual perceptions of what is safe and what is not. How much do you know about this 2-year-old boy's particular need for a sense of safety:

- What indicates to you that this child feels safe or does not?
- Does this child look to you for protection occasionally, often, or rarely?
- What is the family's perception of the child's safety in this program?
- How do you think the family's perception affects the child's feelings of safety?

Abraham Maslow (1970) wrote about levels of needs. His third level after basic physical needs and the need for protection included love and closeness. Children need to feel they belong. They need people who help them feel valued, appreciated, and accepted. Think again about a particular child, a 3-year-old girl. Ask yourself what you know about the child's relationships:

- What indications are there that this child is getting enough caring attention?
- Do I have a relationship with the child? With the family?
- Is there anything that concerns me about this child's sense of belonging in my program? In her family?

Looking at Gender and Age Differences

Do you see a difference between fulfilling girls' needs and those of boys? While many needs are the same whether we are thinking of a baby, a young child, an adolescent, or an adult, age certainly makes a difference in how these needs are met. When you look at needs from a psychosocial point of view as Erikson did, you can see that there is a succession of particular needs, or tasks, to be accomplished as the child grows. The first occurs in the initial year of life and the need is to establish trust (see Attachment). The second task relates to a need to gain a feeling of autonomy and occurs in the second year. Because Erikson was a student of Sigmund Freud, their stage theories relate to each other. Freud sees the first year as the time when oral needs are the greatest and the second year as the time when elimination needs come into focus. According to Erikson, children aged 3, 4, and 5 need to gain a sense of initiative. Because Erickson came from a cultural background inclined toward an emphasis on individualism, it's important to remember that a collectivist might look at this succession of needs related to stage theory very differently.

Implications for Practice

Pay close attention to how well children's basic needs are being met. Also notice how long children have to wait to get their needs met. Using a stopwatch will help you come up with a cumulative record of minutes spent waiting. We've talked about basic needs in the section on Body. We have also talked about children's sense of security and a feeling of belonging in a number of other places in this book. Here we will focus specifically on Erikson's notions about the need for a sense of initiative.

To help children gain a sense of initiative, they need the freedom to make choices within a rich environment that presents an array of opportunities. Equally as important, they need help to appreciate the consequences of their choices and to respect the choices of others. For example, when a child decides that the truck she chose isn't as interesting as the one another child chose, she has to learn to live with that choice or learn how to negotiate a swap. A sense of initiative comes out of feelings of empowerment, believing that it's okay to act, to take a stand. To do that requires confidence, a strong sense of self, a predisposition to think that most things you do will be okay and when they aren't you're not devastated. Feeling that you are a valued member of the group and one who makes an important contribution generates a sense of initiative.

The tried and true adage in early childhood about the importance of making clear to a child the distinction between your ongoing positive regard for the child and your disapproval of the child's behavior (Criticize the behavior, not the child) is an important one. If children come to see themselves as naughty, unworthy, clumsy, dumb, or in any other negative way, then a sense of constructive initiative will not develop as fully as it might otherwise.

Sometimes young children display initiative that is well intentioned but has an undesired impact; that is, they often do the wrong thing for the right reason. For example, a toddler wanting to show affection to a baby may squeeze the baby vigorously and make her cry. A 3-year-old helping to clear the table may drop food or dishes on the floor. It is important in responding to these initiatives on children's part that adults show pleasure and approval for their intentions, and then help them learn to do it better.

You could say that initiative is a willingness to "have a go," the confidence to take risks and meet challenges. In their responses to children, adults teach them whether or not it's okay to try.

OUTSTANDING QUALITIES

Focusing on outstanding qualities instead of deficits and weaknesses makes a big difference. Each child brings strengths, talents, and gifts to the program. Pay attention to what those are. Is a child particularly creative? Sometimes creativity is underappreciated and even mislabeled because children who think and behave in unusual ways are likely to get into trouble. Creative urges do not always lead to being neat or considerate of others. Creativity means breaking the rules, and breaking the rules can get a child a reputation that isn't helpful to the child or his or her self-esteem.

You may think of asking yourself about a particular child, "Is this child gifted?" Avoid that question. Instead ask, "*How* is this child gifted?" And ask it about every child in your group. The term *gifted* means to some that the child is outstanding in an academic sense, or perhaps has a special talent for math, music, or art. We want to suggest that all children are gifted if you take a broader look. In his book *Frames of Mind*, Gardner (1983) outlines seven areas of giftedness. Later he came up with an eighth. He called these areas:

1. linguistic intelligence;
2. logical-mathematic intelligence;
3. spatial intelligence;
4. musical intelligence;
5. bodily-kinesthetic intelligence;
6. interpersonal intelligence;
7. intrapersonal intelligence; and
8. naturalist intelligence.

You can use Howard Gardner's areas of giftedness to look at the outstanding qualities in children by considering the following questions. Think about a 5-year-old boy and ask if this particular child has the outstanding ability to:

- Use language effectively by being especially sensitive to sounds, rhythms, and meanings of words? Does the child like to play with sounds and words? This ability shows up when a child is particularly articulate and can explain ideas, tell stories, make up poems, or use metaphors.

- Think mathematically by seeing patterns and showing skills in logical thinking? This ability shows up when a child constantly seeks out and solves math problems encountered in daily living and play. The child also asks questions and explores the environment in ways that show that he formulates and tests hypotheses.
- Notice spatial relations and details of objects in the environment? The child with this quality can conjure up mental images and perceive them accurately. He can imagine how an object will look if moved, turned, or transformed. This ability helps a child notice and reproduce fine discriminations among similar objects. Drawing may be a talent.
- Understand, appreciate, and create music? Can the child produce sounds varying in pitch, rhythm, and tone? The musical child may be noticeable. He hums, sings, makes up songs, and is attracted to musical instruments. He may be able to reproduce a tune he has only heard once.
- Use his body skillfully? This is the athlete, craftsperson, or dancer. It's easy to notice the 5-year-old who can ride a bike without training wheels. This child was the toddler who could be found constantly taking apart furniture, twirling though space, or climbing on trees (or kitchen counters).
- Notice the subtleties of other people's behavior by reading moods, understanding intentions, inclinations, and desires? This child not only notices what's going on with other people, but is influenced by it. This is the child who pats you and asks what you are sad about before you even realize you are sad.
- Recognize his own feelings, motives, strengths, and desires? This child may seem self-absorbed, because self-understanding is important and fascinating to him. This child may also use self-understanding to relate effectively to other people.
- Recognize patterns in nature and differences among natural objects and life forms? This child is drawn to nature and shows interest in rocks, insects, plants, and animals. Classifying collections of natural objects may be fascinating even at a young age.

Looking at Gender and Age Differences

We assume that you might be tired of going through every section looking at every age group and both genders by now; that is, if you followed our instructions and started with the letter A and read through. But this one is worth switching genders, just to see if you have preconceived notions about which collection of talents is more likely to be masculine and which feminine. We hope you will be able to think of particular children who do not fit the stereotypes of gender-related qualities; for example, the girl with mathematical gifts and the boy who is gifted with a high degree of interpersonal intelligence. Also look for examples that go against stereotypes within the eight categories, such as a boy who is a dancer and a girl who is an accomplished athlete.

We also want to mention age differences here. Babies don't fit in the examples above very well, yet babies do have outstanding qualities. Think about babies who are particularly good at "hooking" an adult's attention or are very good at quieting themselves. Think of toddlers who are particularly adept with language or ones who seem passionate about moving to music. Maybe with babies it's more appropriate to think of predispositions toward certain kinds of gifts, but it's just as important as it is with older children to notice them, celebrate them, and nurture them.

Implications for Practice

Of course, once you become acutely aware of a child's outstanding qualities, you want to consider how to act on them. That's part of the planning process. Here we just want to point out that although it is natural to pay attention to what a child is good at doing, don't go overboard. Most children don't need your attention to follow their own pursuits in areas where they excel and are interested. You want them to keep their intrinsic motivation and avoid getting hooked on your attention. When their primary motivation becomes getting attention, they end up performing for others rather than following their own inclinations. Also, the child may come from a family where the cultural imperative is to stay out of the spotlight. The family may not want their child to stand out as an individual and use talents and strengths to gain attention or recognition. They may, however, be pleased to learn of ways in which their child's talent or outstanding quality serves the group and keeps him or her connected to it. This is a significant example of the importance of honoring differences and avoiding trying to make all children fit the same mold.

PLAY

Traditionally, in the view of early childhood educators, play has been seen as the best way for young children to learn. There are many different definitions of play, and that is one of the things that makes it complicated to write about. What is play to one person may not be play to another. Play is usually joyful, but not always. Play often involves creativity and the use of imagination, but not always. Play allows the child to make the rules, but usually only to a degree. Play can be thought of as activity for its own sake, without an aim or product in mind, but not all the time.

Most people who have thought a lot about play come down to a view that it is impossible to categorize any activity as play or not play, and that there is a continuum with "play" at one end and "not play" at the other. Much of what happens in an ECE program falls not on the ends of that continuum but somewhere between. Most people feel that is the way it should be. Play as joyful experiences where the child has considerable control over what happens is critically important in supporting development and learning, whatever the age of the child. A child who doesn't play or who plays only in a very limited way is likely to be a child whose development and learning are restricted.

Play, like so many other concepts we are writing about in this chapter, is affected by age and the developmental achievements and challenges that characterize the particular child. In addition, the child's temperament or style of interacting with the world impacts on play, as do the opportunities for experience and playing with others. Cultural and family background also have an important role. For example, some parents may have very fixed ideas about what types of play and play materials are appropriate for girls and for boys. Each culture has its own traditional games and ways of playing.

In the past, many early childhood professionals looked at play as progressing through some developmental stages, ranging from solitary to parallel to associative to cooperative. It was commonly believed that very young children only engaged in solitary play, and only as they got older were able to play together in a truly interactive way. This was perhaps because, when these ideas were developed, people didn't have much of a chance to see very young children (babies and toddlers) in groups with other babies and toddlers. We now know that even babies engage in short bursts of interactive play with each other, so play doesn't develop in this logical progression. However, it is safe to say that, in general, the older the child the more likely there is to be sustained cooperative play.

Children who have disabilities or developmental delays may have some restrictions on the ways they can play, but play is just as important for them as it is for their typically developing peers. In fact, it could be argued that it is even more important, so that they gain feelings of confidence, competence, and control over some aspects of their own experience. Play can provide them with opportunities to show initiative. These children may need more support and encouragement to play. Sometimes adult intervention may be called for. All children need plenty of opportunities to play using whatever skills they have.

There are some misunderstandings about how valuable play is and how it supports development and learning, especially how it helps children to be ready for school skills, such as reading, writing, and math. Practitioners can play a major role in helping parents to value play, while at the same time valuing the views the parents have.

So, to find out about play, think of a particular 4-year-old girl and ask:

- How does this child like to play? What does she like to play with?
- Are there any kinds of play that she avoids? Do I have ideas about why? Do I need to be concerned about it?
- How do the child's parents view play? Do they value it?
- Are there issues relating to the child's cultural and family background that affect her play?
- Does this child play alone sometimes, with other children at other times, in keeping with her age and developmental level?
- Does she have any physical, mental, or emotional challenges that restrict or impair the ability to play? What strengths does the child have that will support play?

You may want to ask yourself:

- What are your own attitudes toward play? How do you see it in relation to the aims and goals of your program? What role do you think it plays in children's learning and development?
- Think about the play experiences you recall from your childhood. What kinds were the most special? Do you have any ideas why these were the most enjoyable?
- Are you clear about the links between play and the skills children need to succeed in school and life?
- How clear, powerful, and persuasive are you about the role of play when you talk to parents and others about its importance?

Looking at Gender and Age Differences

Play lends itself to thinking about both gender and age differences. A short observation in an ECE program where children are playing will show that what boys choose to play with is usually different from what girls choose. The types of play vary too. Age is a huge factor in how children play. Infant play involves exploration and depends on the skills the infant has. Think of the non-mobile infant's limited exploration compared to the crawler who gets into everything. Contrast that with children standing at easels dabbing at each other's paintings, laughing as they do it. Then think about four children in the dramatic play area who are organizing their pretend play by assigning roles, creating a situation, and even coming up with a plot.

Implications for Practice

If you observe that boys and girls make different choices about what to play with, consider how you might broaden their horizons. If only boys are in the block area and only girls are in the dramatic play area, you can change that by making simple additions. Put small figures or even doll furniture in with the blocks. If girls still aren't drawn to play with the blocks, think about why. Maybe the boys who play there are too rowdy and noisy. Or maybe blocks are perceived as boys' toys or the block area as a boys-only area. Of course, you don't want to get the boys out forever, but it is possible to create girls-only time in the block area. Just announce early that from 10 to 11 o'clock only girls can play with the blocks. Put up a sign to remind them and then enforce the temporary restriction. Lure boys to the dramatic play area by being sure you include male clothing for dressing up. Sports caps, helmets, and hard hats as well as uniforms, men's boots, shoes, and ties are some possible additions. Also consider putting real water in the play sink or play dough on the play table. Or suggest that the dramatic play area could be a space ship or an outdoor campsite and ask who wants to redesign it.

In a mixed-age group, think about how you can make an environment that is suitable for all the ages without limiting experiences for anybody. For example, if babies are present, you need a way for older children to do puzzles, play games with small parts, or use construction toys with many pieces without babies interfering. In family child care homes, adult-size tables or benches allow older children to put materials out of reach of younger children. One children's program used a playpen to separate the babies from the games of the older children, not by putting the babies in it, but rather encouraging the older children to climb in and play.

Make environmental adaptations to support play by children with disabilities or developmental differences. For example, children with severe visual impairments need a predictable environment so they feel free to move around safely. Changing the arrangement, even moving a piece of furniture, means they can't find their way around without bumping into things. Children with auditory challenges have trouble understanding language in a noisy environment, and language can be an important part of play as children interact with each other. A child in a wheelchair needs space to maneuver.

QUESTIONS

We're thinking here literally about the questions children ask. This section looks at mental skills from another window. Although we are focusing on questions, we aren't excluding preverbal children. Just because a child isn't talking doesn't mean that child doesn't have questions. They just aren't expressed in words. Babies and toddlers ask questions by getting involved: What makes the ticking sound in a clock? What happens if I drop this? How high can I climb? Where is mom? What we're talking about here is getting inside a child's mind to try to see what he or she is thinking, especially about the things that are confusing. Think about a 5-year-old girl and consider some of the questions she might be asking. Then think about a toddler boy and reconsider the same list:

- Does this child have one or more burning questions that are on her mind? (For example, she may be wondering about death and dying, even though the question never comes out in words.)
- Do the burning questions the child may have relate to some event in her life or that she knows about?
- Does the child ask these questions? If yes, how?
- What other kinds of questions does the child have (expressed or not)?
- If the child doesn't talk, or talks only in a limited way, how do you know if she has questions?
- Does the child ask or indicate in some way that she doesn't understand something?
- Are some of the child's questions related to things she is particularly interested in and wants to find out more about?
- Can you see this child playing out some of her questions in symbolic ways?
- Does this child ever ask questions that show she is beginning to use critical thinking? "Why did you do that?" is an example, although such a question might be heard mistakenly as a challenge to adult authority.
- How often do the child's questions show that she is trying to make sense of something? "Why does it do that?" is an example.

- If this child doesn't ask questions, is that because in her family questions are discouraged?

It is important to realize that questioning is a cultural behavior. In some cultures children are taught not to ask questions. Barbara Rogoff (1990), in her studies of child rearing in Guatemala, explains something she calls guided participation, which is how a child learns from infancy on to be part of his or her own culture. She explains situations where a child is expected to learn by observing adults and not asking questions. That's a contrast to a culture where children are expected to learn by doing, and where questioning is valued as a learning tool.

You not only want to find out what questions the child is asking, but also what questions the family has about their child, about the program, and about the child in the program. Being open and making time for the family on an ongoing basis makes it easier for the family to ask these questions.

Looking at Gender and Age Differences

Do you perceive general differences between boys' questioning and girls' questioning? If there are some differences, are they in the kinds of questions or what the questions are about? We aren't thinking so much about the kinds of questions that challenge authority. Would gender make a difference to those kinds of questions? You should find out about age differences when you go through the list again with a toddler in mind instead of a 5-year-old. Certainly the practitioner has to be a perceptive and sensitive reader of nonverbal behavior for younger children.

Implications for Practice

Cultural differences can be a major factor when exploring children's and family's questions. As mentioned, some cultures don't encourage questions and indeed may even actively discourage or forbid them. Adults may not expect children to learn to think critically and in fact view critical thinking as counterproductive to their goal of teaching respect for elders and other authorities. Questioning an adult may be considered disrespectful. If in your program you see questioning as an important way to gain information, understand the world, and find out how things work, you may run up against what we call a cultural bump. These are the kinds of bumps that need to be discussed rather than applying a heavy dose of parent education to the situation. Find out what the family's view is. See questioning from their perspective. That doesn't mean you have to give up your perspective on the matter.

We, the authors, obviously believe in questions. This book is full of them. It's hard to imagine living and learning without asking questions, but we know it can be done. Honoring diversity is not always easy!

RELATIONSHIPS

Relationships have come up many times in this book. That's no coincidence. We think relationships are of utmost importance to young children's health, well-being, and mental development. Brain research backs us up. Some questions to ask that will help you understand a child's ability to form relationships are:

- How does this child relate to you?
- How do you feel about this child? What is the quality of your relationship with this child?
- What is the quality of the relationship of the child with the family members?

If you have any concerns about your relationship with either the child or the family, the place to look first is at your own attitudes and behavior. Observing yourself in a self-reflective way can help you answer such questions as:

- Are you competing in any way with the family for the child's affections?
- Is your professional knowledge and/or your ability to work effectively with the child a threat to the family? Do they think you're better with their child than they are?
- Are you aware of saying or doing anything that would seem critical of the family in the child's eyes?
- Are you saying or doing anything that would seem critical of the child in the family's eyes?

Recognizing what is happening is the first step to changing it.

We also want to mention discipline and how it relates to relationships. Whatever approaches you use will be more effective if you have a good relationship with the child. The relationship is also a consideration when deciding what to do. The goal for discipline (sometimes called *guidance*) is to prevent or change unacceptable behavior and at the same time guard the child's sense of self and the relationship with you.

You also want to know how the child forms relationships with other children. That subject was discussed under Interactions. Here we have just two questions:

- Does the child have friends in the program?
- How important are the friends to the quality of the child's experience in the program?

Looking at Gender and Age Differences

Think about gender differences in making relationships. Have you opinions or experiences that lead you to believe the skills in making and maintaining relationships are different with boys and girls? Is the quality of the relationships different? Do you have a different relationship with boys than with girls? We're not looking for right answers to these questions. We're not saying that there should or shouldn't be differences. We are just asking you to explore your own attitudes so you become increasingly self-aware.

Age makes a difference. The 6-month-old who is still non-mobile can't do much about forming relationships or making friends except as people approach her and she interacts with them. The 2-year-old can make choices about who to play with, and the 5-year-old can discuss why he makes the choices he does. Although infants can form multiple relationships, too many people coming and going in their lives can leave them with problems with attachment. Attention should be given to the quality and duration of the relationships that infants and toddlers form. Of course, as children grow older, quality and duration of relationships are still important issues, but their horizons expand and they can enjoy relationships with numerous people. Most can move in and out of group situations easily.

Implications for Practice

Relationships and interactions are at the heart of good practice with children and families, so what you learn about each child's relationships becomes very important in providing for that child's experiences. First, think about what you can do to strengthen the child's relationship with you. Can you find ways to get to know each other better? Take advantage of little opportunities, no matter how brief, to relate to each child and to find out more. Many people believe that a primary caregiving system, where each practitioner takes special responsibility for a small group of children, helps relationships to grow. Of course, you have to be careful not to nurture an exclusive relationship where the child isn't happy or can't cope unless the special person is there. Family child care, of course, has a built-in primary caregiving system.

Continuity of care becomes important if relationships are to develop, especially in infant-toddler care. Sometimes in center-based ECE programs children move up to the next group on a regular basis either because they have a birthday or because they have outgrown the room. Sometimes the whole group "graduates" together and they go on to a new room and/or group and new adults to relate to. Because infants and toddlers develop so rapidly, sometimes they experience a number of graduations, maybe as often as every six months. If they have begun to develop attachments, they feel a wrench of separation as they are separated from the adult they feel closest to. They can go through a period of true mourning. Adults who focus on children's resilience brush off those sad feelings by saying things like, "Oh, they get over it." Yes, they do, but at what cost? There is more and more evidence that continuity of care is a good investment, in spite of difficulties in providing it. Dr. J. Ronald Lally (1995), an American infant-toddler expert who heads up the WestEd Program for Infant Toddler Caregivers, believes that infants and toddlers should have a chance to keep a relationship with one adult or several for their first 3 years. In programs where continuity of care exists, children may move to new physical environments more than once, but the practitioner or practitioners they are used to go along with them. Of course continuity of care is built in to family child care homes unless the family moves or changes providers.

It's not just relationships between children and early childhood practitioners, but also parent–child relationships that are an important consideration. We have said before that probably the most important thing an early childhood practitioner can do is to strengthen the relationship between the parent and child. An approach to working on the strengthening is to support parents and help them increase their knowledge of their child in order to further appreciate individual characteristics and uniqueness. In its simplest form, this means sharing positive information with parents about the child and reassuring them whenever you can.

Encouraging relationships among children means giving them a choice. Relationships are encouraged when children are not pressured to always be together or to cooperate. Relationships arise from choices about being with others or being (relatively) on your own. Adults can help children learn how to be with other children in positive and constructive ways, through modeling, helping children to solve problems when there is a conflict, and supporting them to learn appropriate ways to interact and to assert themselves. Encouraging relationships among children requires adults to let go of idealized notions of the social child. Some children are outgoing and seem to need other children a lot of the time, while others are happiest in a one-to-one situation, and still others seem happy to be on their own. Sort out children's preferences so you know if they are loners or have a limited number of friendships because it's their choice or because they just don't know how to make friends. Make sure that children who lack skills to make friends have many opportunities to learn them. Some will need an adult there to help them learn. This is where facilitating and direct teaching come in.

SPECIAL ISSUES

We have chosen to look at two special issues. One involves children with special needs and the other involves children who endure hardships. Gunilla Dahlberg (1999) says Sweden has tried to move away from a simple classification of "children at risk" and "children with special needs," related to a deficit concept, with the role of institutions being to compensate for that deficit. Instead the emphasis has been on early childhood institutions for *all* children. The approach we are taking here is in line with Dahlberg's assertion that children should not be segregated from their peers on the basis of their condition or risk factors. In other words, we believe that ECE programs should be prepared to work with (that is, care for and educate) all children, integrating into the program those with identified challenges. In ECE programs in Australia there has been an active policy of inclusion of children with identified challenges for some time. A similar change of perspective appears in the United States in laws related to what has been called special education. The mandate is that special education (which Dahlberg terms "additional support") be carried out in a natural environment. The definition of a natural environment is one where a child would find typically developing peers. In other words, children eligible for special education (or additional support) should have access to ECE programs. Another group that deserves additional support in natural environments includes the children considered at risk because of hardships they endure.

This coming together is not only an advantage for the children being included, but also for those in the program who do not face the same kinds of challenges. Separating and segregating children with particular challenges is a disservice to everybody because all children have things to teach and learn from each other. Inclusion benefits everyone and leads to a more integrated community.

We'll start with children who have developmental differences. Those differences may exist in a single area of development or across several areas. We're talking about what are called physical, mental, or emotional disabilities or delays. In the name of using an image of the competent child, we would like to get children out of the category of extra needy and help people focus on the abilities they have instead of the ones they don't have. We can consider some children challenged in particular areas instead of disabled or handicapped. These children have special rights as a moral mandate, as well as under the law in many places. They may need additional support, but that doesn't mean we can't look at them as competent. No child is perfect—no person is perfect. All have areas where growth and development are more challenging than others. All children have capabilities. Helping them use the capabilities they have and move at their own pace into new areas of capabilities where they have potential is the job of ECE professionals, working in collaboration with others. A team effort is required if inclusion of children who need additional support is to be successful. The team includes the ECE practitioners, families of the children, and specialists who offer support and expertise.

Questions to ask about a particular child who may need additional support to meet developmental challenges are:

- What are this child's strengths and talents?
- What special consideration or assistance does this child need from you and the other children?
- How well does the environment that you have set up work for this child?
- Have you made it easy for the child to access the materials, explore the space, and interact with the other children?
- What modifications might you need to make in the way you handle the essential activities of daily living to accommodate this child?
- What might some particular health and safety issues be that you haven't considered?
- What can the family tell you about how to support, care for, and educate this child?
- What special considerations does the family think need to be made?
- What other professionals are part of this child's life, how can they help support you in caring for and educating this child, and what contributions can you make to their understanding and appreciation of this child?

- How well do the other children and families understand this child's situation?

Of course, some very important questions are:

- What are your feelings and attitudes toward people with disabilities in general, and people with particular kinds of disabilities?
- If you have feelings of discomfort, what might be the reasons, and what can you do to overcome them?

Now we want to look at children who have so much turmoil and hardship to endure that the troubles in their lives affect their ability to relate to others, to learn, and maybe even their capacity to develop. This group is also likely to need additional support in their care and education. We have separated the two groups here because we don't mean to suggest that children who have disabilities tend to come from families in extreme stress or turmoil. Certainly a disability can cause both, but we're looking at a different category of children who have hardships that impact their development. In some cases a child may be in both groups. For example, a child may have a physical disability and may have lived in a series of foster homes, after being removed from a parent who is an alcoholic. What are other examples of the kinds of hardship young children experience? Poverty, discrimination, violent neighborhoods, troubled family life, parental mental illness and/or substance abuse, separations, deaths, divorces, neglect, and abuse are all examples. The list can go on and on. The stress that comes with such hardships puts a strain on the child's coping resources and puts the child at risk for emotional, behavioral, developmental, and learning difficulties and further hardship.

Again we want to focus not on an extra needy child, but rather on the protective factors that help all children reduce stress and overcome hardship. Our information is coming from long-term resiliency studies that show how some children overcome a deeply troubled early childhood and go on to become whole, healthy, and productive adults who lead satisfying lives (Werner, 1995). The protective factors come from the child's own personality, the family environment, or outside support. Just one protective factor can make a difference in outcomes. It's important to remember that. If everything seems to be against the child, but he or she has particular personality characteristics, a supportive family environment, or even a single person who can provide support (whether in the family or outside of it), even one of those factors can make all the difference.

In order to focus on the positive protective factors in children under stress, consider the following questions. Pick a particular child whom you think is experiencing a good deal of stress and consider what you know about:

- The child's personality. What about this child has the potential to draw people toward him or her? Under what circumstances does the child show warmth, enthusiasm, interest, initiative, a sense of self-worth? What helps this child adapt to change?
- The child's family life. Does the family provide for warm, close relationships and maintain some organization and order in the environment and in the child's life?
- Whether or not there is a person in the child's life (inside or outside the family) who has a special relationship with the child, helps the child cope, provides a good model for the child, and represents a support system.

Some children's personalities unfortunately aren't such that they draw people to them, and they may also live in turmoil at home. That's still no reason to despair. Having just one good relationship can make all the difference. If the child has no one to turn to, consider that perhaps you can be that one person who makes a difference. You don't have to be a therapist, but rather just be there for the child by providing a warm, caring professional relationship. If that isn't possible, or even if it is, some children need additional help and support in the form of intervention by community resources or elders.

Sometimes a family is misunderstood by professionals who assume they are experiencing hardship and turmoil that affects the child. If this is a child from a cultural and/or linguistic background that is different from that of the professional, it is possible that cultural differences are getting in the way of the professional seeing the true picture. We caution once again not to judge everyone by one's own cultural measuring stick.

Looking at Gender and Age Differences

If you are reading straight through this alphabet as we have suggested (instead of choosing particular concepts), you've already found out a lot about your gender issues and biases. We hope you are by now automatically looking at how abilities intersect with gender in your mind. What about children living with more than average stress and hardship? Are there connections with gender? Is a girl living in hardship more or less distressing to you than a boy? Do you have ideas about which gender is more likely to overcome the difficulties? Do you have more ideas about how to work with boys than with girls?

Chronological age sometimes becomes less of a factor when looking at certain kinds of emotional and behavioral issues, disabilities, and developmental disruptions. Knowing how old a child is doesn't necessarily tell you what he or she is capable of. You have to set aside any concepts or assumptions that don't match the actual child. Age in months or years isn't a major factor for some children. Concentrate instead on individuals. But do be sensitive to peer acceptance and don't treat a child like a baby whose age level and physical development are beyond infancy. For example, a 4-year-old had difficulty turning the pages of regular books designed for children that age. She could turn pages easily in books designed for babies, but was bored with the subject matter. Her teacher took apart some books she enjoyed, stiffened the pages, and made cardboard books out of them with easy-to-turn pages.

Implications for Practice

Don't consider yourself alone in your endeavors to include children who have special issues and present special challenges to you. Certainly having a creative approach to solving problems will help you meet individual needs and figure out ways to make the group fit the individuals, but you shouldn't see yourself as working on your own. Families have expertise about their own child that you don't have. Use their knowledge! Families can also lead you to resources with specialized expertise beyond that which they or you possess. Use these specialists. On the other hand, you may be the one leading the families to community resources that they don't know about. Also look to other practitioners for support—practitioners who have also included children who need additional help in their programs. Exchanging ideas can be invaluable!

Some policy issues arise that you may or may not have control over, but you have to recognize the impact they have on your ability and that of your service to carry out inclusion of children with special issues successfully. Having an adult–child ratio that allows for close and lasting relationships is vital. Responsive, individualized care and education is a key ingredient and depends to some extent on having a sufficiently small group and a good practitioner–child ratio. When adults spend their days herding large groups of children, many children get lost in the crowd, while others develop extreme behavior in order to be noticed. No child should feel lost or unnoticed, including those whose special issues call for additional help and support.

Because the theme of including children with disabilities appears throughout this book, the implications for practice are to be found scattered throughout. Here, we review some suggestions made in other places. Think about how to adapt the environment and equipment to fit individuals. Put yourself in the particular child's shoes and see how it feels to spend time in the environment as you have it set up for the group. You can even get down at the child's level to literally take his or her perspective.

Adapt the essential activities of daily living (caregiving routines) so they work for the individual and use them as times to build relationships. An example of an adaptation comes from a family child care provider who had a child with a severe visual impairment in her home. She noticed that when the food she served was the same color as the plate, the child had difficulties feeding herself. She bought new plates of several colors and from then on selected the plate that contrasted most with the food to be served.

Communicate naturally all day long, especially with children who don't talk or who lack other kinds of communication skills. Provide mobility for children whose typically developing peers have it, so they can get around also. Provide reasonable limits for all children, but pay particular attention to those who are testing and pushing the limits. Enforce the limits firmly, but gently. Do everything you can to help the child have a sense of security. That means everything from carefully positioning a child who has physical or neurological disabilities, to supporting children emotionally who are dealing with separation issues, to arranging the environment carefully for a child with visual impairments or one who uses a walker. Make provisions to support participation when learning opportunities arise that some children can't fully take advantage of. While still calling parents' attention to accomplishments of typically developing children ("Look how well he's walking now!" or "He did a hundred-piece puzzle today!"), tune in to the less obvious but equally important accomplishments of children who make any progress in smaller steps ("He held his own spoon today").

TEMPERAMENT

One child is full of vim and vigour, racing headlong through life and embracing new experiences as they come along. Another child is slow paced, hangs back from new experiences, and is always cautious. The two children have different temperaments, and it is likely the differences showed up when they were babies. The word *temperament* describes personality characteristics that are behind patterns of behavior—the typical ways that children have of responding to emotional events and new situations. It also includes the way they control or do not control their impulses. Think about this situation. A child has a birthday and the parents hire a clown to come to the program. Although most of the group is delighted, there are two children who look a little scared. They hang back. When the clown approaches them, they back away and one hides under a table.

Usually adults can predict how a particular child will behave in a particular situation because they are familiar with his or her temperament. Although three temperamental types were identified by Alexander Thomas and Stella Chess (1968), who did the original research, those three types are made up of differing combinations and degrees of nine traits. Back in 1968, Thomas and Chess labelled the three temperament types:

1. the easy child;
2. the difficult child; and
3. the slow-to-warm-up child.

Like so many other categories, the categorizing of children in this way reflects cultural values. The easy child is flexible, in that he or she adapts to new things, tends to be cheerful, and establishes a predictable routine in infancy. The difficult child (*feisty* is a more positive term) is intense, reacts negatively to new things, is less flexible, and is irregular in routines. The slow-to-warm-up child can be described as cautious, fearful, or shy, and is more passive than the other two. His or her reactions are mild and low-key, but mood is often negative. This child adjusts slowly to new experiences. People use the information about temperaments to help parents and professionals understand differences in children and learn to accept and respect the differences. A good match between adult and child temperament makes living or working with the child easier.

Think about the three types as labeled and described. Is one more appealing to you? How much do you think your preference is related to your culture? Cultural values show up when labeling or describing temperaments. Even though we know we should value and respect differences, who wants a difficult child? But is a difficult child always considered difficult? When we look across cultures we get a different idea about these categories and labels. In some situations having what Thomas and Chess called a difficult baby is an advantage. For example, in times of famine in Africa, the difficult/feisty babies are the ones most likely to survive. Their intense demands probably get them more food than the less demanding babies. In Israel, early childhood care and education professionals are drawn to difficult/feisty children. Their active, intense, and demanding personality traits fit the national interest. Maybe feisty children aren't so difficult in Israel because they are less likely to be cooped up in small playrooms than in some other cultures and instead spend lots of time outdoors with plenty of space to move around. In the United States, shy withdrawn children are considered socially immature, whereas in China children described the same way are considered to be advanced.

So, labels aside, let's look at the nine dimensions that Thomas and Chess determined make up temperament. Think about a particular 3-year-old boy and the extent to which this child exhibits the following:

- *Activity level.* What is this child's normal activity level? Is this a child who is always in motion? Or is he more often still?
- *Rhythmicity.* How easy is it to predict when this child will be hungry, tired, or need to use the toilet? Does he have some kind of rhythm or schedule or is this child's expression of physical needs unpredictable?
- *Distractibility.* How easily is this child's attention captured by what's going on around him? Does he have the ability to keep focused and concentrate?
- *Approach/withdrawal.* How does this child respond to a new person, thing, or situation? Is he drawn to new experiences? Does he readily accept new foods, for example? Or, is his first inclination to reject anything new?
- *Adaptability.* How does this child handle change? Does he adapt quickly, slowly, or not at all?
- *Attention span and persistence.* How long will this child stay focused on an activity? How long does this child's interest ordinarily last? Does the child persist in the face of difficulty?
- *Intensity of reaction.* What is the energy level of this child's emotional response? Is he loud when happy or unhappy, or are expressions of feelings muted?
- *Threshold of responsiveness.* How much does it take to get this child to respond? Some children respond to the slightest change while others seem oblivious.
- *Quality of mood.* How often is the child cheerful, in a good mood, compared to either showing no emotion or acting unhappy or unfriendly?

Think about your own temperamental traits. Reflect on how you would answer the questions above about yourself. Think about a child you have trouble getting along with and assess that child's temperamental traits. Do they match yours? Sometimes we have problems getting along with people who are just like us, and other times we have problems with people who are very different from us. After doing this little exercise did you gain any insights about yourself, the child, or the issues between you?

Looking at Gender and Age Differences

Review the nine traits and see if you have a different feeling about seeing them in a boy than in a girl. Are some more appropriate to your concept of femininity? Do some traits fit better with your idea of masculinity? How able are you to accept what you may consider feminine traits when they show up in a boy? What about the reverse? What about your own gender and personality traits? Do they match up with your ideas and preferences?

There are, of course, age factors in temperament. Temperament applies across the age range. If you aren't used to newborns, you may look at several and wonder how temperament can show. It doesn't take much observation to see that newborns are different from each other in many ways, including wake-sleep-activity states. Some sleep a lot, others are wildly active a good deal of the time (usually accompanied by crying), and still others are quietly alert more than others. Some respond to the least little thing, while others seem able to ignore all sensory input except extremes. Of course, when you are looking at newborns you have to realize that temperament isn't the only thing that influences their behavior and makes them different from each other. One sleepy baby may have had a hard birth and be temporarily exhausted and subdued. Don't take that as a temperament trait. Experience has to be taken into account. As infants grow it becomes apparent that they differ in amount and type of bodily movement, how regular or irregular they are in being hungry, sleeping, and eliminating, how easily they adjust to change and accept new people and things.

Temperament follows a person through life. Infants grow into toddlers and show the same temperaments. But remember that as children grow they learn and change. The shy 3-year-old may blossom into an outgoing, confident 4-year-old when he gets used to the setting and has a secure relationship within it. We don't want you to take temperament as a limiting factor, only as one of the many lenses through which to examine, explore, and begin to understand a particular child's behavior.

Implications for Practice

When you understand temperamental differences, you may be less inclined to make value judgments and consider some children as having behavior problems. For example, if you know that some children naturally move around a lot, you can avoid a possibly unwarranted label of *hyperactive* or ADHD (Attention Deficit and Hyperactivity Disorder). Further, with knowledge of temperamental differences you can figure out the best ways to deal with the behaviors that need altering or managing. Temperamental traits require you to individualize your program in order to meet the needs of both the very active child and the one who moves slowly if at all. The child who tends to withdraw in the face of something new needs patience and multiple exposures over time until the unfamiliar becomes more familiar and acceptable and he is able to adapt. The low-intensity child may try to indicate something is the matter, but does it in such a mild way that it isn't taken seriously. On the other hand, the high-intensity child may express so many dramatic feelings that it is difficult to determine what is important and what is just a trivial matter. Recognizing the differences in these two children helps you deal appropriately with each. The child with a low threshold for noise, light, or temperature needs attention to the environment if sensory overload is not to affect her behavior negatively. The high-threshold child needs adult attention when something is bothering her but she isn't conveying that there is any problem. Say she takes a hard fall and gets right up and keeps playing. She may need medical attention, but if you don't investigate, you may not realize it. The highly distractible child may need some environmental modifications to allow him to be able to concentrate. The child who is hard to distract may be difficult to manage, especially if low distractibility is combined with high persistence and the child's goal is to do something that is unacceptable, such as play with something dangerous.

The way practitioners respond to each child's temperament can make a difference in social development and self-esteem. Certainly a lack of acceptance and any negative messages that go along with that can be a detriment to the child. But we're not saying to just put up with whatever the child brings either. Any trait can be both an asset and a liability, and sometimes children need support and guidance so that temperament works for them instead of against them.

UNDERSTANDINGS

We've talked about knowledge and mental skills, and also about questions. This section focuses on how things appear to young children, what puzzles them or doesn't make sense. The implications are about how to help them make sense of the world. So much of the world is a mystery to children. For example, we say "Don't touch, it's hot" and then we touch the coffee cup.

Adam at 3 or 4 made up a little poem that his mother wrote down in her journal. It said, "The moon follows me and nobody else. He sleeps on my porch. I think he likes me." That poem is typical of an egocentric point of view; that is, a child sometimes can only see his or her own point of view and can't relate to anyone else's. It is true that when you look at the moon it seems as though it is looking back. And it does seem to follow you. Also, Adam made the moon into a person. He didn't conceive of it as a dead hunk of rock. Piaget's main interest was in children's misunderstandings, and his legacy to us is plenty of information about how children see things differently from adults (1926/1930). Knowing something about that subject can help guide awareness of what is unique about children's understanding of things and how it might relate to their personal experiences.

It's also important to recognize that although Piaget saw children's understandings as a progression toward logical thought, that's not the only way to look at them. Take a look at what Piaget called animism; that is, believing inanimate objects are alive and have humanlike qualities. Adam's understanding of the moon is an example. From Piaget's perspective this belief is faulty logic. It's to be expected, but it is immature thinking. He didn't consider the fact that a number of mature people in the world have a different understanding and see everything in the world as embodied spirit, from rocks to mountains. That is part of their belief system and, for some, their religion. If we are to honor diversity, we must not judge their thinking as immature, even if we look at the world in a very different way.

Again, an example from Adam at age 5. He got in the car one morning; his mother backed out and felt a bump under the car. It turned out that Adam's kitten had hidden in the wheel well and was now lying dead on the pavement with a tire mark across its midsection. Adam took it calmly. He figured it was only a matter of taking the kitten to the doctor and getting it fixed. His mother explained why that wouldn't work. Adam didn't believe her and insisted that they at least try! His mother gently refused. He ended up having his first tantrum. That was the beginning of Adam trying to grasp the idea of death, its meaning and its implications for him. For weeks the questions came as he started to understand. When told that people grow old and die, he checked out each old person he knew. "Will Grandpa die? Will Grandma?" Then he started thinking about people who weren't old, but were on the way. "Will you die, Mommy?" When he finally realized nobody is exempt, he asked, "Will I die?" Adam didn't talk much, but he was a deep thinker. He thought about death for a long time and finally found a way to deal with his fears. One day he said to his mother, "Well, everybody dies, but then I think they just get born all over again." Adam invented reincarnation, little knowing that the idea is the basis of more than one religion. He worked on understanding death until he finally came up with a comforting thought and stuck with it. His obsession with death ended.

A last story about Adam from his mother's journal. Adam had nightmares and often shared them. One day he explained that he had figured out a way to control the bad dreams. He said, "I put my dream on a television set and then I just changed the channel until I got a picture of me climbing on the jungle gym at preschool. Then I wasn't scared anymore." Adam's understanding of dreams was that they were a form of reality that could be managed, controlled, and changed. That understanding is not part of his culture, but some cultures would agree with Adam that dreams are a form of reality and can be lived as such.

So to begin to know how a particular child understands the world, think about a 4-year-old boy, and ask yourself these questions:

- What situations help me see how this child's understanding of the world gives him power?
- What situations help me see how this child's understanding of the world differs from mine?
- What has this child said that leads me to know how he understands the world?
- Are there any major life events that are affecting the way this child understands the world?
- Are there any particular experiences that are less than major but that affect the way this child understands the world?
- What is unique about the way this child understands the world?
- What can I learn from the family about how this child sees the world?
- What are the belief systems in the family that differ from mine, and how do those belief systems affect this child's understanding of the world?
- What does research say about how children understand the world?

Looking at Gender and Age Differences

Part of this section focuses on the development of logical thinking. Consider whether you believe boys are more inclined to logical thinking than girls and, if you do, what are the implications for your practice? Think also about whether you are better at figuring out what one gender is thinking than the other. The examples given are of a boy. Can you think of examples that help you peek into the head of a girl and see what her understandings are? Would they be different because of her gender?

Whether gender matters or not, obviously age does. We can only guess what goes on in the mind of a baby, except as we can read body language. Even when that baby can talk, we have more to work with, but words may not exactly express the child's understanding. We have to guess and interpret from paying attention to behavior. Knowing what the researchers such as Piaget have come up with can help, but we still must approach children as individuals and not try to fit them into someone's theory, disregarding everything else. We also have to take culture into consideration because it affects how the child is being taught (whether consciously or unconsciously) to understand the world.

Implications for Practice

Well, we are back to relationships once again. To know how anyone understands something we have to know the person, and we know people best when in a relationship with them. We learn through observing, interacting, and communicating with them. So what do we do with what we learn? Do we correct what we consider misunderstandings? That depends on what the misunderstanding is. If a baby thinks her mom is gone forever, helping that baby understand that it isn't so is very important. Not that words alone will do it, but repeated experiences will. Once the child comes to expect the return of the parent you can assume she now understands that the separation is temporary, not permanent. If a toddler doesn't know a stove is hot, certainly that misconception needs correcting. If a 4-year-old thinks that the moon is alive, it wouldn't hurt to help him pursue more knowledge about the moon, but only if he is interested. Of course, answer any questions he has. Piaget would have just kept listening to him though and supported him in creating more poetry without telling him he was wrong about his egocentric view or his view that the moon had feelings.

If a child's understanding of the world is that it is always chaotic and unpredictable, you can help that child understand there is order and meaning through the way you set up the environment and through the experiences you provide. If the child understands only violent aggression as the way to solve problems, you can certainly give some alternative understandings. Providing an interesting, rich environment with plenty of opportunities for the children to follow their interests and desires helps them fine-tune a myriad of understandings that they come with and acquire in your service. Think of approaches you can use to stimulate children's curiosity and inventiveness. Remember that understandings don't just reside in the mind. The child comes as a whole package—mind, body, and feelings are all connected. Understandings relate to all three.

VOICE

Language as it connects with voice starts with the baby's first sounds, crying, although before long the cooing and babbling start. Crying is voiced communication, and an effective way to get across the urgency of their needs. We're using the term *voice* in several senses. We not only mean the ability for children to express themselves in their unique ways and be heard, but we also will deal with language in general, going beyond what is voiced to include other forms of communication. Crying is accompanied by facial expressions and body language to help get the message across. These beginnings of communication develop into spoken language over the first year of life. Of course, long before their first word, babies understand much of what others say to them, and in the first years they continue to understand more than they can say. When they say their first word, oral language begins, but communication still continues throughout life in numerous ways that don't rely on words or that go beyond them.

Literacy is another form of communication and a part of language. Literacy can also be considered to begin at birth as babies begin to make sense of what they see, hear, taste, and touch. At first they have only pure sensation coming in, but processes in the brain take the input from the senses a step further and turn sensation into perception. The typical course toward literacy depends on visual and auditory perception; that is, the child learns to distinguish one shape and one sound from another.

Learning to read can be compared to learning to ski. You get the children used to snow before you set them up on skis and, if they are babies and can't yet even walk, you do it slowly because they need to develop their bones, muscles, and sense of balance. You introduce them to snow slowly over time and do it in such a way that they come to appreciate snow, not fear it. Your goal, of course, is to get them to love it! You engage children with literacy in the same way, by giving them many chances to develop their perceptual, mental, and fine motor skills. They need a good deal of exposure to and practice with language before they begin to understand that the sounds they hear can be represented by marks, marks that they can read and marks that they can make. They also need a wide variety of experiences to begin to understand words that they will eventually read.

We are strong proponents of children learning more than one language. We wonder why second language learning starts so late in the educational systems of our two countries. We would like to see second language learning for English speakers start in ECE programs. Ideally all children could begin a second language early, but children who grow up in an English-speaking country and whose home language is not English are in a different situation from the native English speakers. If they retain their home language and add English to it, they have the advantage of having native abilities (or nativelike abilities) in two languages. But that is a big "if." Overwhelming numbers of children lose their home language when they learn English. We want to look a little closer at children whose home language is not English because their second language learning is often misunderstood.

It is commonly assumed that children readily and quickly pick up a second language and do so without any psychological or emotional consequences. Both of those assumptions are questionable. First of all, children take time to develop in their own language, and it only makes sense that they take time to develop in a second language too. Twelve years is what the experts say it takes for acquisition of one's native language. A child who is learning a second language may sound fluent in conversation rather quickly, but there is much more to language learning than being able to converse casually. A child who is learning a second language can't be expected to develop faster in that one than in the first language. Second, there can be enormous consequences if children whose home language is not English are put into an all-English environment too soon with no support for their home language. As mentioned before, loss of home language is common. Language and identity are closely tied, so language loss has implications for identity development, which can have huge psychological and emotional repercussions.

Issues of identity and empowerment are reasons that we chose to place the discussion on language under Voice. When we talk about a person having a voice, we are talking about power. How do we give children and their families a voice? One way is to support the language children bring with them into the ECE program. It may be hard for the practitioner whose only language is English, especially if that practitioner sees the urgency for the child to acquire the dominant language of the country. It's even harder if the parents also urge early English acquisition. Nevertheless, we hope we have convinced you of the importance of children continuing to develop in their home language.

Some questions to ask concerning a particular child's language development are:

- What is this child's first or home language, and how well does the child use that language?
- What kinds of supports and experiences will help the child develop further?
- Will this child benefit from learning a second language at this time? If so, is that possible?
- What evidence is there of early literacy skills, such as print awareness and familiarity with books?

- Is the child interested in books?
- Does this child experience him- or herself as having a voice in the sense of having the power to be heard?
- Does the child state opinions, ask questions, and talk about feelings?
- Is the child using his or her voice to state opinions, ask questions, and talk about feelings in harmony with the family's ideas about children and their respect for elders?
- How do you feel about the ways the child chooses to use his or her voice?

Gender and Age Differences

You may perceive language differences between boys and girls. Whether you do or not, it's important to consider equity issues. Do you speak more to one gender than the other? Do you speak differently to girls than to boys? Become aware of what unconscious gender messages you may be giving as you use language with children.

Most people do change their language according to a child's age. The natural inclination seems to be to speak more simply to babies and to repeat a lot, although some people avoid what they consider "baby talk" and speak to children the same way they speak to adults. Both ways work. The important thing is to remember that babies are receptive to language long before they utter their first word. Talking is a good investment. Listening is an equally good investment.

Implications for Practice

The implications relate to communication, language, literacy, identity, and empowerment. Communication is one of the most important things you teach, and you do it every day in everything you do. You facilitate communication when you try hard to read all the signals children give you, not just the verbal ones. Becoming aware of your own communication is part of this. Watch to see how often your words and your body language are at odds with each other. Be careful to try to make them match, or children become confused. One example comes from a story of a teacher who said to a child she had always treated coldly, "I love you." The child picked up an incongruity and said clearly and directly to the teacher, "I wish you'd tell your face." Apparently the teacher's facial expression contradicted her words.

Language is, of course, part of communication. Putting things into words is a way children increase their language abilities. Talking to children, even the ones who don't yet talk themselves, increases their receptive language skills as you give them practice in understanding what you are saying. Listening to children encourages them to produce language themselves. Talking children through conflicts and problems helps them see how we can use language to think and to sort things out.

Exposing children to written language of all forms helps them develop literacy skills. Write notes to parents, get-well cards to sick children, cards for birthdays, congratulations cards, and cards to celebrate new babies. As children come to understand the purpose of reading and writing, they'll be more ready to do it themselves. Put children in what has been called a language envelope, which means including language in everything you do. Surround them with language.

Don't teach language in a formal way. Some people worry about correcting every mistake and making lessons out of language learning. Children do better when adults carry on authentic conversations with them instead of giving language lessons. That's where listening comes in. A conversation is two-way. If one person does all the talking, it isn't a conversation. Help children learn turn-taking in conversations by being a good conversationalist yourself.

We have made a strong appeal for supporting a child's home language. That may not be easy if you don't speak the languages of the children in your program. But, it all starts with an attitude. If you truly value the languages your children bring, they and the families will pick up your respect. Accepting the language the child brings contributes to the development of a sense of identity and helps empower the child.

WILL

By *will* we mean "a constructive force that guides intuition, impulse, emotion, and imagination toward complete realization of the self" (Assagioli, 1972, p. 8). Self-determination could be another way of saying what we mean. Motivation is a little different but is also along the same lines. *Motivation* comes from a Latin root meaning "to move" and can be defined as that which energizes, guides, and sustains behavior. We're talking about the kind of inner energy that helps people take determined action, make physical and/or mental efforts to reach a goal or overcome an obstacle. The will gives one power to choose; to express oneself without inhibitions or defenses and also to control impulses and delay gratification. Energy from the will helps bring about changes in self, others, and situations.

We chose a simple word to express this kind of energy, not one usually used in early childhood education books. We realize that the word *will* is used in a number of ways and has a number of connotations, even though we don't acknowledge that often. Willingness is the opposite of willfulness, for example. A strong-willed child can be hard to get along with, even if we are saying that willpower is a good thing.

Here is an incident featuring a strong-willed child. *Stubborn* was how the adults who worked with him saw him. This 4-year-old boy was hard to get along with because he was often contrary. Once he got something in his mind he hung on to it like a dog with a sock in its teeth. The adults just hoped every day that they wouldn't have to come up against that willpower; it was formidable. If he didn't want to do something he would hold out forever as long as someone was trying to make him change his mind. This boy showed himself in a different light one day when a teacher took a cardboard box out of a cupboard and set it on the table to look for a padlock she thought was in there. She picked through it and found a padlock right away, in fact, lots of padlocks; but there were no keys. She dumped out the box on the table and there amid the assorted junk were scattered numerous keys. What a mess! She sighed and started to put it all back in the box. The boy sprang into action. "I can find the key," he said. He started sorting through the jumble. It took a long time to find the right key, but he persisted. Then he picked up another lock and started searching for its key. Pretty soon he had the locks all laid out on the table and began in earnest to match keys to each lock. No one told him to do it, but he stuck to the task even though it took him the rest of the morning. When he was finished he called the adult and stood there grinning proudly at his accomplishment. For the first time the adults could see the value of this child's stubborn streak. His persistence paid off!

When we look at this boy's will we can see a combination of several dimensions of temperament. He is low on distractibility, high on attention span, and high on intensity. When used for constructive purposes, a strong will is regarded positively. The trick is to develop skill in using the will. Paying attention to the boy for his positive action is a beginning to helping him develop some skills.

Think about the willpower or, if you prefer, *motivation* of a particular child:

- How often does the child take on challenges and work to surmount obstacles, and how much energy does he or she put into confronting challenges and obstacles?
- Is the child persistent?
- What kinds of challenges and obstacles does the child confront?
- Under what kinds of circumstances does he or she display the kind of energy, direction, and ability to remain goal-oriented, all of which indicate will or motivation?

- Is the child's will a source of satisfaction to him or her, or does it seem to be more of a problem?
- To what extent does the child make the kinds of choices that show that he or she has specific goals?
- What kinds of goals are they?
- What seems to motivate the child?
- To what extent does the child depend on adult attention, including praise and rewards of other types, to keep him- or herself on track toward a goal?
- What are some other forms of adult support that work to help the child find the means to set goals and the energy and direction to carry them out?
- How does the family feel about the child meeting challenges and confronting obstacles?
- How does the family feel about the child's ability to make choices, set goals, and carry them out?
- How might what motivates the child relate to his or her culture?

Self-regulation is also part of the picture. Think about this child and ask:

- What ways does he or she use to calm down when overly anxious or excited?
- How well does he or she control impulses?
- How well does he or she express emotions (verbally or other ways)?
- What ways does the child use to cope when frustrated in getting something desired or needed?
- What ideas do the parents have about self-regulation and how do they fit with your ideas?
- How do you feel about and respond to strong-willed children, especially when they defy you? Is that related in any way to how strong-willed you are?

Looking at Gender and Age Differences

When you think of someone with a strong will, do you usually think of a boy? Or of a girl? Does who you think about come from personal experience with someone, or do you naturally relate gender to willpower? What about willfulness? What about determination? What about stubbornness? How about self-motivation? Is that a gender-related characteristic in your mind? Impulse control? Expression of emotions? Self-regulation? Where do cultural differences come in, or do they? Although a strong will may show at birth, other aspects such as impulse control, emotional expression, and coping skills come with age as children develop and learn.

Implications for Practice

Motivation for learning comes automatically when children can follow their own interests and passions. Will provides built-in motivation. It isn't easy to work with a group of children in ways that allow each to pursue his or her own interests, but it's worth striving for. Of course, it isn't always just individual children following their own passions, but often children naturally put themselves in groups. A child may have no interest in a particular project or activity until other children become interested. Passion can be contagious.

Some children have a lot more built-in motivation than others. Most young children, for example, have strong urges to explore any environment they find themselves in. Some children with certain disabilities may lack those strong urges, or if they have them, find it hard to move around enough to engage with the environment. Enticing children can help. Make the environment irresistible and at the same time figure out ways that make it easy for every child to engage with it

Teaching children delayed gratification is a big step toward helping them enjoy their lives, be productive, and get along with others. It's natural for young children to be in a hurry to get something they want or need, but they can learn about the joys of anticipation. Certainly looking forward to an event or outcome can be even more satisfying and exciting than experiencing it. Just being aware that delayed gratification can be taught in small steps is important and can help when you are faced with an impatient child who is hard to get along with. Starting in infancy, children can learn to wait. Not all the time and not long when they are infants because waiting is hard. These are just beginning lessons and it is more important that they get their needs met in a timely manner than it is that they get used to waiting. We're not suggesting that you teach them to be happy waiting in line for hours every day, or that you deliberately delay their pleasures time after time. We're only suggesting that learning sometimes to put off something that may even feel urgent can be good for children when it balances with plenty of experiences that they don't have to wait for.

Taking turns not only helps children learn about the needs and wants of others and the importance of balancing them with their own, but it also teaches delayed gratification. Planting a garden is a good way for children old enough to be involved to learn about delayed gratification. The rewards come way down the line, but the pleasure of working for them can be worth the wait.

XPLORATION

We acknowledge that we're cheating here, by pretending that *exploration* is spelled *xploration*! The term *exploration* is often used alongside the term *play* when early childhood professionals are talking about valuable experiences to support development and learning. Exploration is about finding out, discovering, figuring something out yourself. A poster about babies developed by one of the authors shows a 1-year-old leaning over the side of his high chair, staring intently as he carefully pours his cup of juice on the floor. The caption reads: The world's greatest scientists, explorers, and physicists wear diapers!

Exploration starts in infancy, as babies seem driven to use whatever skills they have to figure out how the world works, and development leads to more and more ways to explore the world around them. The early childhood years are characterized by a lot of physical exploration; that is, getting in there with your hands, feet, your whole body, as well as your mind to figure things out. As children become verbal their exploration is enhanced by their ability to ask questions, speculate, and hypothesize.

Whether it's a baby or a 5-year-old, exploration is most powerful when the child is in charge, when he or she feels secure enough and sufficiently confident to act on the world to find out more about it. Exploration both satisfies and fuels curiosity and a drive to know more, both of which are characteristics of successful learners.

Exploration in ECE programs is often noisy, messy, and, to an uninformed observer, may look like just "messing around." Parents may need to be reassured that real investigation and learning are taking place.

The child who is reluctant to explore may be one who has not been rewarded for initiative and risk taking, who has been encouraged to be passive and compliant. These children need support from sensitive adults to learn to be confident explorers. Other children who are hesitant to explore may be those with disabilities and other special needs. Sometimes they just don't have exploratory urges and need help to get going. At other times they may lack the ability to move through the environment enough to display exploratory behaviors. In either case, these children need additional help if they are to reach their exploratory potential.

You may want to ask:

- How much does this child explore? How does he or she explore?
- What interests this child, particularly just now?
- What messages has this child absorbed about exploration and risk taking?

- Are there likely to be any conflicts between messages the child is getting at home and in the program about exploration?

You may want to ask yourself:

- What are my attitudes about messy exploration?
- Am I a risk taker and explorer myself? How does that impact on what I provide for the children I work with?
- Am I clear about what children are getting out of their exploration, and am I able to articulate this to parents?
- Do I have a drive to learn and know more about children in general and about the particular children I work with?

Looking at Gender and Age Differences

Some people are convinced that boys explore more than girls. If that is true, it may be that the boys are encouraged more, or even given unconscious messages about adult expectations of them. Or it may be that certain environments are more enticing for boys than for girls. In any case, be sure that girls are allowed and encouraged to explore as much as boys. Mobile infants, those who crawl, are the original explorers and might be said to be the world's greatest, at least for their size. Of course, there is individual variation, but the very young are famous for getting into everything. They do it every chance they get. They don't just move around, but also take things apart to see how they work. Tasting, touching, banging, smelling, and poking are all exploratory behaviors. Even biting can be done in an exploratory mode, although it still hurts when teeth engage with flesh and needs to be prevented. As children grow out of toddlerhood they don't give up exploring, but they add many more skills, so physical exploring takes its place among a variety of approaches to learning about the world.

Implications for Practice

Sensory exploration is a way children learn, so they need to spend a good deal of time in safe and interesting environments that invite exploration. Safety is a big issue. If it isn't safe, they can't freely explore. Safety doesn't just focus on physical well-being but takes in the emotional realm as well. If a child doesn't feel secure, exploratory behaviors may be inhibited. Security needs may be heightened for a child with physical or neurological challenges. Some children need to be supported physically in an upright position so that they can use their hands. This can be done with cushions, or they may need to be strapped into a chair. Space to explore is one factor, and time is another. When days are filled with planned, purposeful, adult-organized activities, children may get the message that it isn't okay to explore. They may actually experience uncomfortable consequences for doing something unplanned. Children not only need space and time to explore, they need *things* to explore. Of course, toys and equipment come to mind, but don't forget that nature is full of wonderful things for children to learn about through exploration.

One issue that comes up regularly when discussing exploration is the objections of some adults to messy exploration. Whether it is a cultural or personal issue isn't really the point. The point is to honor differences, even when you don't agree with them. If you are a person who thinks mud wrestling on hot days is the most wonderful activity you can imagine, we urge you to listen to a parent who thinks it is disgusting, immoral, and downright dangerous. We're not telling you to give up mud wrestling, only to talk it over with those who disagree and sort it out among yourselves.

YEARNINGS

Yearnings is an unusual word, not one we use ordinarily, at least in our early childhood vocabularies. We are thinking of yearnings as passions or longings, so the term relates both to intense interests and intense "wants." We think it is important for the practitioner to know about both the child's yearnings and the parent's yearnings in relation to the child.

Empathy will help the practitioner think about what a child coming for the first time to an early childhood program yearns for. He or she probably yearns for familiarity in place, smells, sounds, sights, and, most important, in people. Sometimes we forget that in terms of their basic human feelings and what prompts them, young children are in many ways more like us than they are different from us.

A child whose life is very busy and filled with changes may yearn for peace and quiet, for calm. A child whose life is filled with lots of people may yearn for some time alone. A child whose life is filled with busy adults may yearn for someone to just take time with her. Often what we don't have enough of is what we yearn for. The point is that children's deep yearnings are in many ways simply human yearnings, and we must not forget that.

Young children have passions too. A baby who has just learned to stagger a few steps on his own is very likely on the verge of developing a passion for walking. A toddler who has just learned to walk up and down a step successfully may have a passion for doing it over and over because it feels so good to be successful, as will one who has just mastered using a spoon. Among the many kinds of opportunities and experiences offered in early childhood programs, children will develop passions for particular ones—for painting, or blocks, or music, or engaging in elaborate dramatic play in the home corner, or riding bikes around and around, or making up silly words. Sometimes passions are intense interests that are shared by several children. As an example, typically many 4- and 5-year-olds develop a passion for dinosaurs, many for fairies, and others for superheroes. Sometimes, as with adults, passions are lifelong, and sometimes they are brief. Yearnings and passions in children are about their individuality, the essence of them as unique human beings.

Admittedly, as is the case with adults, not all passions in children can or should be encouraged or even allowed. For example, some toddlers develop a passion for sinking their teeth into other people's flesh. Some 4-year-olds develop a passion for the shock value of certain words when used in the presence of adults.

With regard to parents' yearnings for their child, as practitioners get to know families, they will come to have a picture of how the family sees the child, and what they hope for that child. Some of these yearnings may be quite specific, for example, wanting very much for their child to develop a love of music or art, to graduate from college, or wanting their child to become an accomplished athlete. Other parents will be less specific, but almost all parents want their child to have close friends, get a good education, eventually do work that is fulfilling, experience the joy of family, be constructive community members, and be safe and healthy. It is important to know what parents want, and what their priorities are. It is also important to get a feeling over time of how realistic their expectations are, and the extent to which they appreciate the unique individual that is their child.

So, you may want to find out:

- What does this child yearn for?
- What are this child's current passions?
- What do the parents want for this child? How realistic is this? Where did these yearnings come from?

You may want to ask yourself:

- What are my own professional yearnings and passions? How do these impact on my work?

- Do I have an idea of the ideal child? If so, how would I describe it? Does it affect my work with children? If so, how?

Looking at Gender and Age Differences

Are passions, yearnings, and longings different for boys than for girls? How do you know? Would such a difference matter to you in your work with children? If yes, how? The examples above show some of the differences in yearnings that can be attributed to age. It would be easy to assume that yearnings and longings become more sophisticated as the child grows older, but that isn't necessarily true. Some lifelong yearnings carry over from the early years and may still be basic rather than more sophisticated. Some are specific to the age. For example, few adults yearn to sink their teeth into human flesh, although that may be a burning yearning in a toddler.

Implications for Practice

What practitioners do once they know about children's yearnings is in some ways pretty obvious, but difficult to generalize about. What you do about them, in general, is to take them into account in your interactions, in your plans, in what you offer to children, and in what you talk about with parents. Yearnings are about people's uniqueness, what makes each of us special and engaging and human. The interests and passions of the people, both children and adults, in an ECE program are what give it its color and richness.

Sometimes in our efforts to be developmentally appropriate, or to be seen to be educating children, to be accountable, and to be getting them ready for school, it's easy to lapse into the "tried and true" when it comes to practice. This means doing those things that come to mind first when we think of early childhood practice—blocks, home corner, messy play, puzzles, familiar songs and finger plays, group time, Lego and Duplo, sand and water, play dough, and so on. Being aware of yearnings should help us to move beyond the predictable, the obvious, and contemplate the unorthodox, the unusual, the unexpected.

Yearnings are reminders about individuality, and putting knowledge of yearnings into practice reminds us to relate to each child, each parent as a unique individual. It's a warning to resist stereotypes and generalizations, to be ready to be surprised by people we encounter in our work.

Yearnings is not a category on an admission form or a topic for an intake interview. It's a mind-set to have as we get to know others as individuals, moving beyond, in the case of children, seeing them as a collection of developmental milestones. In the case of practitioners relating to parents, it's about moving beyond categories and even moving beyond viewing them only as parents, and relating to them as people too. It's about understanding them in ways that help ensure that the care and education provided will be in line with the family's hopes and dreams for the child.

ZONES OF PROXIMAL DEVELOPMENT

We've tried so far to avoid jargon in this book. We're making an exception here because the zone of proximal development (zpd) is such a useful concept. The term comes from Lev Vygotsky's work (1978), and we are using it to mean the child's leading edge. Being aware of the zpd, that area where embryonic abilities lie, can give the adult ideas about what kinds of experiences will nurture and support these abilities and help them develop into full-blown competencies. As the child grows, learns, and changes, the zpd moves. It's never stationary, but always sliding forward. That's what leading edges do—they lead.

This view of learning promotes the idea that children learn by trying things they can't do by themselves—things they need help with. This fits a collectivist's orientation. If a child can do something easily all by her- or himself, there's no learning, no cutting edge. Learning is stepping out into new territory and usually needs someone besides the learner. Working in concert with a more competent person is more effective than taking on tasks independently, according to this view. This idea also fits the apprenticeship approach to the teaching/learning process, including Barbara Rogoff's (1990) view of what she calls *guided participation*. It also fits the custom of including children in adult activities, so they learn from people older than they are. Some families include children in all the family activities; that is, they don't have separate adult events, celebrations, rituals, evenings out, or holidays. They also don't have birthday parties just for children, but include adult family members and friends. This way children are not segregated, but rather are a part of everything. Where parents and families include children in their work, their domestic activities, their celebrations, children do some of their most important learning of "work" skills and social skills, as well as getting a picture of themselves as useful and as contributing members of the family.

Think about:

- What knowledge do you have of a particular child's zpd in physical abilities?
- What challenges or new territories is the child ready for, and what will help that child move forward in physical abilities?
- Who might assist the child in making progress?
- What knowledge do you have of a particular child's zpd in mental abilities?
- What challenges or new territories is the child ready for and what will help that child move forward in mental abilities?
- Who might assist the child in making progress?
- What knowledge do you have of a particular child's zpd in emotional development and social skills?
- What challenges or new territories is the child ready for and what will help that child move forward in emotional development and social skills?
- Who might assist the child in making progress?

The idea of the zpd is helping the child stretch to grow, which is appropriate sometimes if you don't get carried away. We can't be stretching every minute. There are times that everyone needs to sit back and rest on their present knowledge and enjoy being good at what they can already do. An example is a family who had children in the primary grades who were learning to read through an approach called programmed reading. Every time they finished books at one level, they were presented immediately with more challenging books. This approach responded perfectly to their zpd. But then the family had a new baby, and the mother brought out all the books she had read to the older children as babies. The older children were greatly attracted to these easy picture books. They delighted in reading at a much lower level than they were capable of. Throughout the baby's early years the older children read and enjoyed books at his level. In school they were challenged; at home they relaxed. The point is to balance the pushing forward with plenty of time to let children do thoroughly whatever it is that they are doing without hurrying them on to the next thing. So we leave this section with one last set of questions:

- What is this child very good at doing and how much time does the child get to spend doing it?
- Does the child feel pushed to learn and develop, or is he learning and developing at his own pace and speed?
- Is learning joyful?

Looking at Gender and Age Differences

Do you have different expectations for learning in boys and girls? Does it seem more important that one gender move ahead faster or more than the other? How do you see age relating to the zpd? All children have a growing edge, although what it looks like is different in an infant, toddler, 2-, 3-, 4-, or 5-year-old. It's also individually different as well, depending on the ability and interest of the child, the family, and/or the culture.

Implications for Practice

ECE programs provide a mix of opportunities that cater to what the children are able to do now and what they are interested in, on the one hand, and on the other relate to what they might want to tackle next. Obviously this might be more challenging with a wide age range in the same group, such as exists usually in family child care. On the other hand, a tremendous strength of mixed-age groups is that children extend each other. In mixed-age groups children have many opportunities to be teachers of older and younger children. Whatever the age range, children benefit when they are provided with materials and equipment, a physical environment, time, and adult support to work and learn together from each other.

We've said several times in this book that providing for future skills and developmental achievements isn't at all the same thing as pushing children to "move on" to the next thing. It also isn't being so locked into what the child development books tell you is supposed to come next that you don't see what the child is actually telling you or showing you about what he or she is interested in. Let children surprise you. And, as has already been suggested, let learning be joyful.

Another implication from this last letter of the alphabet is a reminder about communication. A term such as *zone of proximal development* probably wouldn't mean anything to someone who hasn't studied child development. *The zpd* would mean even less. Using such lingo excludes others, such as parents; the disadvantage is that the meaning isn't shared, and ultimately children don't reap the benefit. One of the most exciting kinds of insights for professionals or parents to gain is to understand clearly a phenomenon or concept that comes from academic or research literature. It is the professional's role not to confuse (or even dazzle) with jargon, but to be a translator so all can share in increased insight and sensitivity to children.

Well, there it is—A to Z! What you have here is only one version of an alphabet of important concepts. We could have done it differently. You and your colleagues might enjoy thinking of alternatives for the letters—concepts that are particularly important in your work with young children and their families.

LOOKING FORWARD

The next chapter is about gathering information and turning it into plans and practice. It borrows from the information in this and the preceding chapters. Although we have been told that practitioners want lists of things they need to listen for, watch for, and ask about, we want to move beyond just checklists. There are systems for collecting and documenting the information you need to create curricula and build plans.

5

Gathering Information and Planning

ISSUES ASSOCIATED WITH PLANNING or programming in ECE environments have been controversial over the years. For example, frequently a few years ago, and occasionally even today, there were some people who believed that either it is not possible or that you shouldn't plan for the youngest children, especially babies and toddlers. Some people who work in family child care resist the idea of planning, making assertions to the effect that doing so "will take the family out of family child care." Some people, invoking the artificial and outdated care versus education distinction, would assert that planning (they would probably use the term *programming*) is appropriate for educational programs, but not care programs. This resistance to planning (the term we prefer to use rather than *programming*) has its origins in what we think are some mistaken and restrictive views of planning, what it involves, and how it affects practice.

Planning, whether for a dinner party, a holiday, or a day or week in an ECE program, involves pretty much the same thing. You use your prior knowledge and experience, think about what you want to happen and what you think will happen. You try to be as prepared as you can be for the unexpected. Planning in an early childhood program requires "thinking on your feet," as you pay attention to how things play out and the reactions. You modify plans as you go and make mental or written notes to help you plan in the future. Like a dinner party or a holiday too, you think about what works well, what you would change next time.

Working as a practitioner in ECE programs involves a continuous cycle of gathering information, planning, gathering more information as you implement the plans and altering them as you work, and using that information for future planning. The purpose for both gathering information and planning is to provide experiences for each child and for the whole group that support well-being, development, and learning. So really, gathering information and planning are part of the same process and are interwoven. In this chapter, however, we have separated them for the sake of discussion, while still affirming their strong connection.

We are also adopting another conventional distinction, namely that between evaluation and assessment. In this discussion we use *evaluation* to talk about gathering information about the program or aspects of it and making judgments and interpretations based on that information. *Assessment* we use to refer specifically to processes for collecting information and making judgments and interpretations about children. However, we see the two as closely related and overlapping.

This whole book is based on working in collaboration with families. This means that families are an integral part of the processes of gathering information, ongoing planning and evaluation of the program, and ongoing assessment of their child. As we indicated in Chapter 2, their perspectives and priorities will sometimes differ from yours, but even when they do, or especially when they do, it is critically important that you know how parents see the program and how they see their child. Families are an invaluable source of information about their child. When practitioners work in partnership with families, there is continual sharing of insights and information about the child. Each benefits from the perspective of the other.

While the daily informal conversations are the most important way to share information, it is useful for practitioners to think of additional ways to encourage parents to share their insights. Sharing journal writing, which is discussed below, is one way. Two additional specific ways that come to mind as examples are to schedule an interview between parents and the people who work with their child several times a year, and to periodically give parents an information update sheet to complete on their child. Better still, practitioners and parents can complete it together.

Parents' interest often goes beyond the direct experience of their child. It helps to maintain collaboration, and the program benefits, when practitioners also find ways to ask parents what they think about the program. Helping parents focus on the various program dimensions discussed in this chapter not only leads to constructive comments and suggestions and helps practitioners maintain an understanding of how the program is viewed by parents, but also increases parents' appreciation of the complexity of working well with children. Because of their greater understanding, they are likely to become more effective advocates for the program. The more information practitioners share with parents, the more they are likely to get back. Some parents will be interested in sharing ideas for experiences for the children and contributing to them themselves. When they discuss with practitioners their children's interests and experiences outside the program, they are adding to the wealth of possibilities for planning.

INFORMATION ABOUT EVERY CHILD AND MORE

Part of planning is making sure that no child is overlooked. It's easy to be distracted by the children who capture or demand your attention and ignore the ones who don't. Some children seem to be practically invisible when in a group. One way to help determine whether this invisibility factor is present is to sit down periodically with a list of the children. Think about each one and see if something stands out about that child that day. If you have time, write a short comment by each name. If you find it hard to think of a comment, that child may be one who is relatively invisible, one whom you may have unintentionally overlooked. Once you realize that fact, gathering information and planning can include ways for you to focus on that particular child so you can be sure that the program matches and supports that child as well as the rest of the children.

In addition to focusing on children when gathering information as a basis for planning and curriculum, it is useful to focus also on particular parts of the day, the overall physical environment as well as specific areas within it, the structure of time, and the carrying out of routine activities or daily living experiences. Targeting these elements or dimensions of the program will, of course, involve focusing on children at the same time, as you look to see how these elements work for the children.

Gathering information using a number of different perspectives will lead to information and insights that are valuable for planning. If all parts of the day are important for children's learning, then practitioners need to look carefully at what is happening throughout the day.

In general:

- Do the children appear relaxed, secure, and happy most of the time?
- Are children engaged constructively in experiences that interest them?
- Do they have choices?
- Are experiences individualized so that, to the extent possible, they meet the needs of each child in the group?
- Are the experiences designed to appeal to the interests and strengths of individuals and groups of children?
- Is anyone being excluded?
- Is there a good mix of challenges and easy, comfortable things to do so that children experience both many opportunities to be successful and the satisfaction of being extended through trying hard?
- Is there a balance of the familiar to provide security and the novel to provide interest?

- Do children have opportunities to continue over a period
  with experiences that particularly engage them? Do they have
  opportunities to revisit these engaging experiences?
- Do children have the choice to withdraw safely for a while, and to
  choose between being with others and being by themselves?
- Do children have opportunities to be with children their own age
  as well as children who are older and younger?
- Are the children supported to feel part of their local community?
- Is diversity of all kinds acknowledged and supported in the
  program?
- In both the set-up of the physical environment and the practices, is
  there appropriate attention to health, safety, and hygiene, while at
  the same time allowing children to explore, experiment, and play?

The discussion and questions that follow are about some of the kinds
of insights practitioners need in order to offer beneficial experiences to
children. This discussion is not comprehensive or exhaustive; for example,
it does not include the detailed questions about the specifics of health,
safety, and hygiene. We are instead highlighting some of the important
dimensions of programs about which it is useful to gather information
for planning. Obviously the categories and the questions within those categories overlap. We have organized the discussion around the following
topics:

- the physical environment;
- organization and time; and
- routine daily living experiences.

The Environment

The environment plays a big role in how smoothly and effectively the
program runs. Think about the total environment, including the materials and equipment. How is it working, in general, for you and the children? What can make it work even better? The environment gives strong
messages about what kinds of behavior are expected. Think about the
difference between a library, a church, a bank, a playroom, and a park.
Each is designed for the behaviors considered appropriate to the setting.
Make sure you plan your setting so that the behaviors expected of the
children are ones that promote their growth, development, and learning. The environment should say "Explore and interact with me." Ideally children should have plenty of access to outdoor environments as
well as indoor ones. Both parts of the environment need careful thought
and planning.

The environment should also say "Interact with each other." One part of planning includes promoting interactions among the children. The set-up of the environment either helps or hinders. Certainly every child should have the choice to be part of the whole group, to play with a smaller collection of children, to play in pairs, and to be alone. Planning has to take into consideration how to promote these changing configurations as well as how to manage them.

What about the child who is always alone? What kind of environmental planning will help that child find someone else to play with? How do you get a wanderer to settle down or into a group? Again, there are implications for the way the environment is set up. Is there a space for the whole group to get together?

Thinking about these questions and then experimenting with room arrangement and reorganizing materials and equipment can make a difference. Is there an area that children tend to run around in rather than focusing on what you've provided there? Do you have noisy areas next to quiet ones, so that children interfere with one another's concentration? Are the toys and materials out of reach of the children so they have to ask for them, or are they out and available for the children to choose?

In summary, and in addition to the questions above, ask yourself:

- Is the space arranged to give children the choice of being together or being on their own? Does it give children a choice to play in groups, in pairs, or by themselves, depending on their inclination that day or that period of their lives?
- Are materials arranged attractively and in ways that invite constructive use?
- Are materials that go together placed near each other, and those that do not go well together (for example, paints and blocks) separated?
- Are there sufficient materials and equipment to encourage cooperation and prevent unnecessary frustration?
- Does the physical environment empower children, whatever their age and ability—that is, does it allow them to do things for themselves as they want to and are capable? At the same time, is that aim balanced with attention to health and safety considerations for the age or ages of the children in the group?
- Is the environment set up to encourage children to concentrate?
- Is there sufficient attention to aesthetics, to ensure that beauty is always present in the physical environment?
- Is the outdoor environment used fully for its special features and opportunities as well as for an alternative space to do things that can be done inside?

- Is the environment sufficiently rich to be stimulating and interesting without being overwhelming and kaleidoscopically busy? Is there too much or too little in it?
- Does the physical environment reflect the lives of the children and families, particularly the diversity within the group and in the local community?
- Is the environment set up in ways that direct children to particular experiences and opportunities?
- Are pathways sensible—that is, does the traffic through the space avoid disrupting children at work?
- In what ways does the environment entice children to explore, experiment, discover, and solve problems?

Organization and Time

It's interesting the extent to which we are used to connecting our essential activities of daily living to time. It's hard to even find words to label these activities without referring to time. When talking about these daily events in our services, we use the terms *lunch time, snack time, sleep and rest time, outdoor time,* and *group time.* Certainly back at the beginning of the industrial age, putting people into a time frame was called for in societies where the goal was to produce factory workers who lived (and died) by whistles and bells. That's not the goal of ECE programs. One goal ought to be to help children tune in to their own body signals as well as adjust themselves to group living. If you are a person used to living by the clock, it might be an adjustment to put that aside and just plan sequences within a loose time frame. Children don't need clocks, but they do need some routine in their daily lives; that is, for things to happen in a predictable sequence. When things tend to be predictable, changing the routine now and then can make for pleasant surprises. As a general rule of thumb, the younger the child the more important are predictability and a routine.

The organization of time in early childhood programs relates closely to the value adults place on giving children choices and encouraging initiative—in short, on their willingness to empower children. Programs that operate according to a strict timetable and those where most or all of the time everybody is doing the same thing are generally not programs that place a lot of importance on children's empowerment.

How do you or the children know when it's right to stop doing what you're doing and start doing something else? In other words, how do you decide to move from one experience to another or one place to another? When do you go outside? When do you eat lunch? Are you tempted to put up a timetable on the wall and then check your watch? Do children really need to learn to look at the clock instead of feeling a rhythm to the day?

Planning for transition times within these environments can make all the difference in how smoothly the day or session goes. How do you plan for stopping one thing and starting another? Do you have an effective routine for cleaning up and does the environment support it? Do you have some strategies for helping children who resist change, even regarding something as predictable as coming in for lunch or lying down for a nap? Then, of course, there are the children who not only resist being left in the morning, but also complain heartily about being taken away at the end of the day. Do you have some plans for those times and those children? Do you use the environment to support you in those plans?

In summary, and in addition to the questions above, ask yourself:

- Do children have to wait unnecessarily?
- Do they seem rushed, or appear not to have time to engage deeply in experiences?
- Does the day or session flow smoothly, with relaxed transitions between one part and the other?
- Is each child's daily routine individualized to fit her or his rhythms, including needs for rest and sleep, food and drink, and exercise?
- Is the structure of the day sufficiently flexible to take advantage of children's moods and energy levels, the weather, and unexpected events, and to make necessary alterations?
- Is there a good balance of a routine that empowers children and gives them feelings of security and at the same time allows for spontaneity and occasional pleasant surprises?

Routine Daily Living Experiences

There is a particular need to look at routine daily living experiences, such as arriving and leaving, resting and sleeping, toileting and diaper changing, hand washing, and eating. These take up much of the time in a children's program, especially with children under age 3. Rather than being times that are rushed through, they can provide opportunities for children to learn, to enjoy one another's company, and to develop new skills and understandings. The physical environment has a major impact on how smoothly and effectively these routines take place. How well does the environment work for the essential activities of daily living, the caregiving routines important for physical health and well-being? Are the areas for these activities clearly defined and well organized?

Do the food preparation and eating areas give messages about what is to happen there? How could eating arrangements be improved so every child's nutritional needs are met in ways that promote social development as well as making eating an emotionally satisfying time?

Are the grooming, toileting, and diaper areas well provisioned and set up so children can take part in the activities?

Is the diaper change area set up so that diaper changing can be a time of intimate one-to-one interaction where you can focus on the child instead of running around finding the things you need? We'd like to suggest that every chance to turn an interaction into a positive experience should be capitalized on. Children get strong messages about themselves and their bodies from diaper changes, and those messages are lasting ones. If they leave the changing table feeling that they have had human-to-human contact, they gain a lot more than just a fresh diaper.

The way the environment is set up plays a role in helping or hindering interactions in daily routine activities.

Think about sleeping. How do you plan for the transition from wake to sleep? Think again about the environment. Are there ways you can change it so it gives calm messages and encourages a slow pace? Can you set it up to support rituals that say, "Slow down now, it's time to rest"? You can't change the color of the walls, but you can give physical cues that convey a sense of peace and quiet, that say "rest time." Lowering the lighting is one such cue; putting soft music on is another.

In summary, and in addition to the above, ask yourself:

- Are these experiences conducted in a child-centered way, allowing children to take responsibility as they are able and want to, so that they build children's feelings of competence?
- Are children moved from one place to another during routines in a respectful manner?
- Do we acknowledge routines as social times, for children to learn from each other, to help each other, and to be together?
- Is sufficient help available to support children? Are children always allowed to use the help and support without feeling they are giving up their independence?
- Are the daily living experiences individualized to fit each child?
- Are daily living experiences offered in such a way as to incorporate the wishes and preferences of parents where possible?
- Is there appropriate concern with nutrition, health, and hygiene in carrying out daily living experiences?

WAYS OF GATHERING INFORMATION

You gather information to use for your planning by watching, listening, discussing (with parents, colleagues, and children), reflecting, writing, and using tape recordings, still photographs, and video to capture what is happening. Some programs make multiple uses of digital cameras and computers. Ongoing evaluation is part of this process of gathering information. It may seem you can do enough by just jotting down notes as you think of things, but you need to figure out a system that includes such devices as checklists and other kinds of forms. Without a way to guide and focus your information collection, you won't be sure that everything is covered and that you are focusing on all the important things. The goal for creating a system is to make it easier for you to link your planning to the information gathered. We created a system for ourselves by using the ABCs of knowledge (see Chapter 4) as one way to make sure that nothing important gets left out as we were thinking about gathering information. You, of course, can think of your own way or modify the ABCs of knowledge to fit your own situation and needs.

There are a number of good ways to collect and record information about the children and the components of your program to help you plan. No one way is best, and most practitioners use a variety of ways.

Documentation

Documentation usually entails the adult, often with the active assistance and contributions of children, creating a record of experiences, sometimes making a collection of records using different methods. Documentation is often used with projects that take place over time and involve a number of experiences, and can be a very effective way of focusing on the process of going about something. This may be done electronically, in written form, through photographs, by making audio or visual recordings, or through visual arts (for example, painting or drawing). The very act of recording what is happening highlights the focus of the project, signals its importance, and often brings to mind new ideas and possibilities for both the adult and the children. Becoming more aware of children's perceptions of what is happening can be very enlightening for the practitioner, a reminder that on occasions what the adult intends and expects that children will learn, focus on, or enjoy, and what actually occurs, are different.

Documentation is also important as a means of letting others, particularly parents, in on what is happening. However, a word of caution—it is easy to become carried away with documentation for its own sake without thinking critically about what the purpose is and how the information can be used constructively. Two obvious examples are that if the main purpose of the documentation is to inform parents about something, then it is critical that the practitioner avoids using jargon and ensures that the documentation is presented in ways that will be clear and interesting to parents. As another example, if the documentation is mainly to support children to record the process of doing a project, say organizing and holding a Mother's Day lunch for their moms, then the methods of documentation should make the information recorded accessible to the children themselves. This would mean, for example, not relying too much on written text.

It is also important to remember that for a child, always having to talk about what you are doing and explain it to an adult who is asking lots of questions, some of which have obvious answers, can be frustrating and boring, and at its extreme may become a disincentive to engagement.

Portfolios

Portfolios are a means of documentation, and they record a child's experiences over a period of time. They are both a context and a foundation for learning. They can be an extensive collection of items, such as written records and media like tapes and photographs, or they can be simply collections of each child's work. A simple portfolio might contain samples of children's work in areas of drawing, painting, and collage, and sometimes photographs of other products, such as constructions in the block corner. Collecting children's work is a popular way of gathering information about strengths and interests. These kinds of portfolios can be a valuable means of recording children's progress over time in a particular area, for example, in drawing. They, of course, are also a handy way to amass and preserve a collection of the child's work for assessment purposes or to give to families.

A more complex portfolio is described by Shores and Grace (1998). This means of documenting each child's development and learning in a portfolio is much more than simply making a collection of a child's work. The complex portfolio includes the child's work and photographs of the child's products, but it can also contain written observations in a variety of formats, samples of conversations on tape, and videos of the child at work and play, all of which are records of the learning and development of the child. A specialized kind of record suggested by Shores and Grace is the learning log. In a way, the learning log is an outgrowth of the kinds of logs kept for infants, a daily record of specifics, such as eating, elimination, sleeping, and other details of the essential activities of daily living. When a child grows out of infancy, the learning log can become a means of keeping track of a larger variety of things—books, materials used, people met, and any number of experiences interesting to the child. If the child is too young to write or draw in his or her own log, the adult takes dictation. Included in the log are the child's thoughts and comments on each entry, including what he or she has learned and what might be the next thing to learn. Advantages of a learning log for the child are the self-reflection aspects as well as ongoing conversations with adults.

Interviews are another portfolio item that Shore and Grace suggest. Interviews can arise from the conversations that occur while making learning log entries. As the adult and child focus on and go deeper into one subject, the conversation goes from being a learning log entry to an interview. Interviews don't have to just come out of learning logs, but can arise easily at any time of the day. The difference between just an interesting conversation and an interview is that the adult keeps a record of it and that record goes into the portfolio. Both the learning log and interviews help ensure that each child has an adult's attention and can have meaningful conversations on a regular basis.

A variation on learning logs and interviews comes from Margaret Carr (2001), who has created something she calls the learning story. She uses a story approach to record and understand children's learning and has taught practitioners to do the same. They learn to remain part of the action while capturing the story of the learning. To do this they must recognize critical moments and memorize the events while taking notes and recording conversations. Facilitating the teaching/learning process while evaluating it means that the practitioner is not taken away from the action. Documenting, evaluating, and assessing become a regular part of working with children. Rather than being objective observers, the practitioner is part of the story, even as he or she is recording it. When more than one adult records the same action or writes the same story, the complexities, inconsistencies, and ambiguities come out. When the child is included in the discussions of the action and the story, the additional voice adds even more complexity, which is regarded as a good thing.

Whatever form or format the portfolio takes, no matter what it includes, it contains a record of aspects of each child's experiences in the program, and can be expanded to include experiences at home as well. Each portfolio is unique, just as each child is unique. In some ways portfolios are the opposite of standardized testing, because their uniqueness reduces the tendency for adults to compare one child with another.

Observing and Recording Behavior

Documentation requires skills in observing and recording behavior, whether formally for a portfolio or the child's record or informally for the adult's information. Learning to look at children through objective eyes is one of the major skills needed for observation, but it isn't enough just to be able to observe objectively. You have to go further and ask regularly: What is the meaning of this behavior? Then you must be able to separate the data on the behavior and your interpretation of what you are seeing. It's important to separate behavior from motive, intent, and meaning. Is the child rubbing her eyes because she is tired, has something in them, or is she imitating what she sees? The important thing is to first notice exactly what she is doing. Understanding the context helps you take the next step, which is to make meaning of what you see. If you know it is naptime, the meaning of the behavior may be more obvious. If a child near her is throwing dirt into the air that may explain the behavior. If she is an infant and someone else is engaged in eye-rubbing behavior, she may be imitating. Of course, usually behavior isn't quite so simple, nor is its explanation.

Being objective is a goal, but at the same time you are a human being and you always bring yourself to the observation. What you see is influenced by who you are, so there is no such thing as 100% objective data.

Anecdotal Records. Anecdotal records can be little notes that are made on the run, or they can be more formal records of things that happen during the day and stand out. Some practitioners keep a pad of paper handy and jot down brief notes so they won't forget. They then expand the notes into formal anecdotal records that record an incident, telling what happened and who was involved. Out of seemingly unconnected notes and records can emerge patterns and answers to questions about a child's learning, development, behavior, or motives. Anecdotal records can also contain quick snatches of conversations, little poems the children make up, or chants they sing while swinging. You can learn something from reading these notes later, especially if you put them together and see a larger picture. You can also use them in a portfolio as language samples or examples of a child's creativity. Keeping anecdotal records on a regular basis by recording something about each child every day or several times a week can tell you which children are getting lots of attention and which ones are being ignored. Anecdotal records are usually written after the fact and based on reflection.

Running Records. Running records of an observation contain a blow-by-blow description of what is happening while it is happening. They should contain a clear description of the behaviors observed. A reader of the running record should see, as nearly as possible, the same scene that you saw. For that reason, instead of saying the child played with a shovel and then refused to give it up when another child wanted it, describe the actual behaviors observed. What exactly did the child do that falls into your category of "played with"? What did the child do when he refused to give it up? Did he turn away, say something, frown, run off, hide the shovel, or hit the other child with it? Describe specific behaviors and sequences of behaviors. "He refused" is an interpretation of behavior, not the behavior itself. A running record observation can be made with or without adult interpretation and speculation about the meaning of the behavior observed; however, when recording both objective data and subjective comments, keep the two separate. Keeping a record of the time makes a difference. You want to know if the child argued over the green-handled spade for a matter of seconds or if it dragged on for minutes. A series of accurate and complete running record observations can help you and others gain insights into a child's interactions, dispositions, feelings, thought processes, and behavior.

Time Samples. Collecting samples of a few targeted behaviors of small groups of children is another way to learn about individual and group patterns. How many of the 4-year-olds in group time were attentive at any given moment? How many were actively involved? Who related to whom, and how?

Incident Reports. Sometimes called event sampling, this kind of report captures a particular type of repeated occurrence from beginning to end. For example, you might observe incidents of hurtful behavior involving a particular child or group of children. These could be like anecdotal records, except that you are focusing on a particular behavior or set of behaviors. Recording what happened before, during, and after the incident can give clues as to why it happened and what to do to prevent it from happening again. Patterns arise when there is a series of incident reports.

Journal Writing. Some practitioners find keeping a journal an important recording device. Journals may contain all sorts of writing—anecdotal records, running records, incident reports. They may also contain drawings or photographs. A journal can be a two-way tool; that is, both parents and the practitioner write in the journal, it goes home with the child each time, and returns to the practitioner the next time the child comes, so everyone gets a chance to write in it. Used this way, the journal becomes an important means of communicating with parents and goes beyond documenting the child's learning and development. The journal can contain learning logs or logs of essential daily activities (for infants).

Photographs, Tape Recordings, and Videos. Capturing the processes and products of children can be useful for practitioners and parents alike. This kind of observation goes beyond writing and helps practitioners take children further into their explorations of specific subjects by recording interviews and conversations about those subjects. Capturing interactions or group conversations on tape can provide valuable records if it is done often enough so that children aren't distracted by the presence of the equipment.

All these are a means of formalizing observations, and are one way of ensuring that you look closely at each child and that you have up-to-date knowledge of development and learning in all areas.

Checklists. Checklists have been used traditionally to assess not only children's development but also dimensions of the program (for example, the environment, health and safety, or routines) or quality in general. Checklists can be useful to remind you of things to look for. No one checklist is comprehensive, and used by themselves checklists have limitations, as those using them tend to see only or mainly what is contained in the checklist and may miss other important information. However, when several checklists are used or they are used in concert with other means of collecting information, they can provide one way of making sure that major areas have been observed.

Assessment of Children

The reason we gather information about children and interpret it is to be able to use it in everyday practice to support their development and learning. Assessment relates to individual children and is used in an ongoing way to help the practitioner be a responsive facilitator of the teaching and learning process. Reviewing the context the children are in is also part of the assessment process. The context includes the environment, plans, and program. Assessment is necessarily complex.

No predetermined checklist sums up a child's knowledge base or skills. We are looking in this book at a different set of outcomes that are much more complex than will ever fit on a checklist.

Both of us have had experience with simplified individualized assessments and we've moved way beyond them. One type takes children out of the learning environment and requires them to demonstrate isolated skills or knowledge out of context. Sometimes what children are asked to demonstrate are things that don't really matter much, but the aim is to prove that the children are progressing and the practitioner is teaching. That's not our idea of assessment. We see assessment as being related to what really matters in a particular program with particular children in a particular community.

We are interested in the degree to which children are learning how to learn and what strategies they use, including how they seek information, ask for help, and interact with others. We want to know their interests and what motivates them, how easily they express their ideas and feelings, what kinds of approaches they take to problem solving, how they collaborate when learning, how they handle uncertainty, what meaning they make, and how they construct knowledge. We want to understand the child's intention in any given situation. We want to find out when they persist on a task, how they use resources, how they become resources for others, when they lead and when they follow.

We are less interested to know if they have reached specified milestones of development as shown on charts. What we want to know is what they can do that may be different from those milestones. How is a child unique? We want to understand the relationship of the child to the environment and others in it. We believe that learning is never context-free.

Assessment is a way to understand each child better, reflect on practice, and plan for that child and for the group. We see involving children in the assessment process as important because it gets them used to the idea of self-assessment. Assessment becomes even more valuable when the information is shared with others in the program as well as the family. Even better is when the family is part of the assessment process. Assessment works best when the person leading it has a relationship with the children that is based on trust and respect.

PRINCIPLES OF PLANNING

We use the terms *plan* and *planning* to talk about the process adults use to think about and prepare for children. Planning, both formal and informal, includes the thinking you do both beforehand and as things are happening, as well as the preparations you make. Making up a batch of play dough before the children arrive is part of planning. But planning happens both when the children are there and aren't there.

Best Guess

For us, a plan is a best guess or an idea about what you are going to do, rather than a firm decision or determination to do something. A plan is a fallback or default position, a basis for variation about what you are going to do. Planning can happen on the spot and be about the next little bit of time as well as about the next week.

Viewing a plan as a best guess helps you not feel locked in to what is planned or allow a plan to inhibit your ability to take notice of what is happening. When you operate with the expectation that the plan will be varied, you open up a lot more opportunities than when you don't. You can also be more responsive. Imagine a situation where the practitioner has planned an experience that makes perfect sense to her, but the children aren't responding at all in the way she intended. Will she stick to the plan or go with the flow? Or imagine a situation where the plan is for the whole group to do something together, but the children are splintering off into collections of children, and some children are going off by themselves. Can the plan be changed to accommodate what is happening rather than forcing the children to all stick together?

Imagine a child who has Down syndrome and has just learned to move around. Suddenly he finds a whole world open to him as he can get to things he is interested in. He finds the playroom of the ECE program fascinating and full of things beckoning him to explore, but the teacher is calling for group time. He is willing to do what she wants, so he allows her to lead him over to the mat. Once there he continues to look around, completely enthralled with the environment around him and not at all interested in what the teacher is doing. Is it more important that he learn to sit still and listen at this time in his life, or is it preferable to let him follow his urges to explore? Is this a time to loosen plans a bit and release him from the spot on the rug? What if the other children get up and leave too?

Elements of Planning

As you would have gathered from reading Chapter 1, we believe that planning has to include more than just activities. Children never stop learning. They are learning every minute of every day. Some of what they are learning will relate directly to your planning and some of it won't, but without careful planning there can be confusion, disorganization, lots of waiting with nothing to do, frustration, disappointment, and sometimes what seems like chaos or even disaster!

Children learn all the time, whether we're planning or not, but what they learn can be desirable or undesirable—that is, they can be learning things we want them to learn or things we don't. An example of the latter is that lack of planning can lead to adults being pulled in many directions, and in that situation children can learn that the best way, in fact the only way, to get an adult's attention is to do something that isn't allowed. Planning leads to a better chance that children's learning will be desirable. Of course, we don't have total control over what they learn. What the adult intends for children to learn and what they actually learn are often different things, and it is good to always be aware of that.

One way to eliminate gaps and risks for undesirable learning is to think about the environment; the routines; the materials and equipment; the children themselves as a group and as individuals; and the interactions that occur among the children, between the children and yourself, between the families and yourself, among the families, between the other adults in the environment and yourself, and among the other adults in the environment. Exhausted? After all, that is what this book has been about so far—thinking about all of those things and using all of the information to plan for children. Remember a program is a mosaic and a mosaic is made of many pieces. All these pieces can fit together into a pattern when we are careful about how we arrange them.

Focus on Every Child and on All Children

We are recommending that, whatever ways you use to gather information and plan, you include in the process mechanisms that ensure that you focus over time on every child and family. How can planning include all children who use the program? Certainly individualizing becomes a mandate when the practitioner is responsible for the care and education of children who differ widely in their abilities. They have to quit thinking only in terms of ages and stages and begin to widen their views and therefore their planning.

Collaboration

We've mentioned before that usually the best plans happen in collaboration with others. Even in family child care, where a carer usually works on her or his own, there should be opportunities to discuss plans with others, share ideas, and gain new perspectives. Members of a team are much more likely to feel a sense of ownership of plans when they contribute to them, and also the program will be richer because of the various perspectives that have contributed.

Including Families

We are advocating encouraging families to also contribute to planning, at least for their own child. In the case of a child with medical issues, developmental delays, or physical, mental, or emotional challenges, the parents must be involved. The practitioner needs more information than what is obtained just through first-hand observation. When planning is collaborative, everybody stands to gain. The family has a body of knowledge that the practitioner lacks, while the practitioner's training gives him or her a body of knowledge that the family probably doesn't have.

Families may have ideas and resources to contribute to the whole program, and there should be a variety of ways available for those families who are interested in doing so.

Ongoing Evaluation

Part of planning includes ongoing evaluation of the plans and the program. We've given you many, many questions to ask, both here and in Chapter 4. You may wish to use some of those questions to create a process of ongoing evaluation that fits your context. Good practice comes from:

- wisdom about the particular children and families you work with;
- understanding yourself;
- cultural responsiveness;
- inclusion;
- community;
- parents as partners; and
- ongoing reflection, dialogue, learning, and informed risk taking.

We will say again that we think you need to create your own methods and instruments that are specific to your program, group, and community. Ongoing evaluation happens when there is a culture of critical reflection and methods for recording observations of both children and practice that are used as a basis for future plans and practice. Keeping track of children's development is part of this ongoing assessment. This doesn't just happen once in a while, but continuously.

PLANNING SYSTEMS AND FORMATS

Settling on ways to collect information about children and understanding the principles behind planning lead you to the next important steps. You have to ask yourself at least two very big questions:

1. What sort of system am I (or are we) going to use in order to have in place an ongoing planning-evaluation cycle?
2. What format works best to actually record the plan?

Let's take the first question. There is no one best way, but the kinds of decisions individuals or groups of staff need to make include the following:

- How frequently will we make a plan and what is the rationale for that decision?

- Who will take main responsibility for the planning? Who will contribute? How can we ensure that everyone involved feels ownership of the plans?
- How do we delegate responsibilities when there are two or more practitioners working together? Who decides and what is the basis for the decision? Is the way we do it the best way to ensure that practitioners are using their strengths and talents and, most important, that the program works well for the children?
- How can we make sufficient time to use the information we have gathered and make plans?
- How will we ensure that we are evaluating and revising the plans as we go, depending on how things are working and what the children are telling us about what they are interested in?
- How will we blend together plans for individual children and for the group as a whole?
- What are the ways that we can involve parents in planning the curriculum?

The way you actually write up the plan is up to you, and there are many resources that contain suggestions for planning formats. All of the thinking practitioners we have known have altered, or sometimes drastically changed, the way they write up their plans as they gain more experience. There are many good ways, and no one best way for all. However, our view is that whatever method you use to document your plans, the important features of planning are illustrated in the formats used. We summarize them below as a reminder.

What are the characteristics of a good planning format?

- It encourages practitioners to think about and plan not just for activities but rather all dimensions of the children's experience: the environment, interactions and relationships, the organization of time, the structure of the program, the indoor and outdoor environments, the daily living routines, provisions for play, as well as special experiences. In fact, these might be categories to use in a planning form.
- It also includes planning for collaborative relationships with families; in other words, plans are not restricted to just the direct work with children but encompass relationships and interactions with families as well. This could also be a category for a planning form.
- It supports planning for individual children, for small groups, and for the group, and encourages strong links between what is provided and what is known about each child.

- It encourages practitioners to think about their aims and goals, and serves as a reminder to ask themselves "Why am I doing this?" or "Why am I doing this in this way?"
- It invites ongoing comment, suggestions, critique, and alterations to future plans.
- If it is meant to be a way to inform families about what is happening and to invite their input, then it is written up in such a way that it has meaning for them.
- It includes blank spaces to allow for unexpected events and alterations.
- It is looked at critically on a regular basis and altered as a result of critique.

There are many resources available that give advice about these systems and provide ready-to-use forms and suggestions for other ways of collecting information and planning, and it is useful to refer to these. We believe, however, that to be effective, you have to take forms developed by others and make them fit your program. We can't know what will work for your program without knowing you, your program, your families, or your community. Rather than creating forms that might be seen as a "one-size-fits-all" standard, we have opted to give you guidance that we hope will encourage and assist you to develop your own systems and forms. The information in this book and in other resources will help you begin to develop your own forms and systems for collecting information that will form a basis for your planning and your practice. We are purposely leaving that up to you.

LOOKING FORWARD

In the concluding chapter, which follows, we suggest some of the main features of a program that translates sound plans into practice in ways that are compatible with the ideas in this book.

6

Action Based
on Collaboration

W E HOPE THAT THIS BOOK HELPS YOU to think about your practice in a different way. We finish by sharing in the following pages some of the most important features of our shared vision of an early childhood program that we would want our own children to attend.

Each type of setting and program (child care center, preschool, or family child care home) brings with it some constraints, challenges, and obstacles, as well as particular strengths. When different program types work well with children and families and support children's development and learning, they may look different, but they have a lot in common. A similar point applies to the age of the children and how they are grouped; that is, whether in mixed- or same-age groups. In other words, the programs and ages may be different, but our vision for programs for babies is very similar to our vision for 4-year-olds; our vision for a group of 2-year-olds is similar to our vision for a group in family child care or a child care center where children range in age from babies to 5-year-olds. This chapter focuses on common qualities in early childhood programs, regardless of the setting and age of the children. Of course, the particular richness and color of the program come from the people in it and the setting.

IN THE END, IT'S ABOUT CULTURE

We think of certain common qualities as the culture of the program. We have chosen the term *culture* deliberately, because culture is something that pervades every aspect of life, whether it's the life of an individual or the life of an early childhood program. Culture is there, whether we acknowledge it or not, whether or not we are even aware of it. Culture is not permanent or static but rather is always evolving. It can change gradually over time. It is both major and obvious elements on the one hand and small and subtle elements that are difficult to identify on the other. We want to describe briefly some interrelated characteristics that contribute to a culture of:

- thinking;
- joy;
- environments that empower;
- linking care and education; and
- relevance and authenticity.

A Culture of Thinking

Adults are thinkers, always reflecting on and critiquing what is happening, wondering about things, and thinking about how they can do things better. They see themselves as learners, and enjoy the intellectual challenges of the work. They know there is always more to learn. Of course, they are also confident about their practice, but at the same time open to new ideas, debate, alternative ways of doing things, compromise, and constructive criticism.

This inclination to think isn't just about individuals but is shared— there is a culture of sharing thoughts, concerns, and questions, debating issues, and an appreciation that doing so usually brings better results than working in isolation. Creating a culture of thinking has implications for both the kinds of people who are hired to do the work and for the way the program operates. Adults who work with children need to be people who always want to learn more.

It isn't enough to just get together a group of people who have these qualities. In our vision the workplace nurtures these qualities. This means that there are professional development experiences to give people exposure to new ideas. The schedule allows for time to discuss and debate, reflect and plan, and there are procedures in place to resolve conflicts in constructive ways.

This culture of thinking translates into aims for and practice with children. Children are encouraged to think, solve problems, extend themselves by accepting challenges, work in collaboration with others, and appreciate their own and others' talents. It is so important for adults to remember that children learn more from what adults do than from what they say. In other words, adults become master learners themselves who model the joy of learning. The adult as learner provides living examples for children of strategies for learning, including how to expand knowledge and solve problems.

A Culture of Joy

Most people who have had opportunities to visit a large number of ECE programs will say that they can tell within minutes of walking in the door whether or not it's a place where they would want to be if they were a child or where they would want their child to be if they were a parent. For us, much of that impression comes from the extent to which a sense of purpose and pleasure is evident. Children and adults are engaged, and there is an overall positive feeling. People are enjoying themselves and feeling comfortable and secure.

This does not mean that there are never tensions, struggles, frustrations, disappointments, even sadness and anger at times. These are emotions that occur whenever human beings, whether adults or children, have meaningful relationships and encounters. A culture of joy means that overall there is a positive feeling about being part of this community and, on balance, far more positive feelings than negative ones. A culture of joy means more smiles and laughter than tears, more singing than shouting, more dancing than running away, more hugs than reprimands, more giving than snatching, more yeses than nos. For us, a culture of joy is sometimes lively and boisterous, and also brings with it intervals of peace and serenity.

It is difficult for us to imagine a place where children are mostly joyful when adults are not; that is, children's happiness is affected greatly by the feelings of adults. However, the opposite is not true. Just because adults are feeling good doesn't necessarily ensure that children are. Adults who focus on children and who do so with a sense of satisfaction and pleasure create a setting where children flourish. Needless to say, adults whose aim in a children's program is to make life easy for themselves at the expense of children's learning and development don't necessarily contribute to a culture of joy for children.

When we use the term *joy,* we don't just mean fun, excitement, and entertainment. Adults aim for much more than that for children, including the satisfaction that can come from engaging seriously with a problem, overcoming an obstacle, exercising some self-control, dealing with conflict constructively, or managing frustration. These things are important and satisfying for children but not necessarily fun. They can be a source of joy, however.

A Culture of Environments That Empower

The physical environment, as well as the operation of the program, sends a message of welcome and empowerment to both children and families. Information is displayed for families in a variety of ways so that they are kept up to date with what is happening and, more importantly, so that the message "what happens here is your business" is conveyed continually and in a variety of ways. For us a feeling of light and space and openness is inviting and comfortable.

This empowering environment for both children and adults is flexible, invites engagement, and is, at the same time, organized, so that things can be found. For example, something as simple as having a place for each child's belongings is empowering for parents, or perhaps more accurately, not having one is disempowering, requiring the parent to search at the end of the day for the child's belongings. For both children and adults, security and empowerment are built on predictability, the assurance that places and routines will be familiar rather than changing constantly.

Part of this assurance and empowerment comes from feeling confident that you know what the rules and expectations are. One of the authors, at a time when she was using family child care for her children, felt somewhat uneasy when she overheard a family child care provider say in a professional development session that it really annoyed her when parents just walked in the door without knocking at the beginning or end of their child's day in care. Another said that she thought it was most inappropriate for parents to go into her kitchen and open the refrigerator to get their child's bottle. Other carers at this session said that they didn't mind parents doing this; in fact they found it helpful. The uneasiness that the author felt was because what was expected and desired in her care situation had not been made clear, and she wondered if she was doing something wrong that she didn't even know about. Having too many rules and procedures restricts freedom and is disempowering but, at the same time, having expectations of how people will behave and not making those clear is equally disempowering. The same goes for children. In relation to both families and children it is worthwhile for practitioners to examine their rules and their expectations, to see if they are relevant and appropriate, and where there are expectations these are made clear and people are helped to meet them.

We see an empowering environment as one that contains equipment and materials that invite initiative and engagement. A variety of materials and equipment is available for children to choose, physical environments are comfortable and attractive, there is sufficient space and time to get involved, and what is available is flexible and lends itself to a variety of uses.

A Culture of Linking Care and Education

In our vision, adults enact an understanding of the inextricable connections between care and education. The two, care and education, are woven tightly together in the minds of the practitioners, and in the organization and implementation of the program. There is appreciation of the truth that young children are learning all the time, not just at the time adults might label as educational. Every opportunity is taken to help children learn how to be in the world. Practitioners appreciate that it is in ordinary everyday events that children do some of their best learning, because that is learning in context.

You could say that desirable education happens when care is done well. *Babysitting* is a term that is used pejoratively to refer to early childhood care and education programs, usually to indicate that nothing more than basic care is happening and the only goal is to keep children safe and healthy. Whatever the program is called and no matter how minimal the goals, when children are with wise and sensitive adults who appreciate their tremendous capacity for learning and their unbridled curiosity, learning and teaching are happening continually in an unobtrusive gentle way, as problems are solved, investigations undertaken, challenges met, questions asked, relationships established and strengthened, skills learned, experiments conducted, and discoveries made. And these things are just as likely to happen in daily living experiences such as dressing, washing, resting and sleeping, packing away, eating, toileting and diaper changing, as they are in times of the day or experiences that are labeled as educational.

You could also say that desirable care happens when education is well done. An early childhood program that calls itself an *educational* program still must provide care for children and the quality of that care relates to the quality of the education. This principle can perhaps be illustrated most effectively by looking at an extreme situation. Effective education is hampered if children are starving, sick, in pain, or exhausted. Only when needs are met can education be effective. And besides, when we think of care we think of more than basic needs—we think of looking after the well-being of the whole person. And that involves education. That's why we have used the word *inextricable*, because in our minds there is no way to separate care and education. Both necessarily occur at all times.

A Culture of Relevance and Authenticity

The most effective learning happens when there is a real reason to learn something, when it links with something the child already knows, when it fits his or her interests and extends them, when what happens inside the early childhood program links with the child's life outside. This is another reason that a standard, one-size-fits-all prescriptive curriculum does not make sense as a way to support children's learning.

Learning in context and learning for a reason are important whether we are thinking of babies or older preschool-aged children. Another way of describing this is that learning happens best when it is intrinsically motivated. Artificially introduced learning experiences, such as object permanence exercises, or just memorizing the alphabet for the sake of it, or practicing large motor skills in a structured way, are not nearly as effective as ensuring that opportunities to learn these things are embedded into the context of children's daily experience in a rich learning environment. Learning to make a salad because a salad is on the menu for lunch, learning the name of a particular bird because she is building a nest outside, learning the route to the mailbox because there's a letter to be mailed, learning what your written name looks like in order to find the hook for your jacket, learning to put on socks because your feet are cold, learning to negotiate the use of a wheelbarrow with another child to take soil to the new garden—these are the important lessons for young children.

The dimension of relevance reinforces the idea that each program will be unique, in as much as it reflects the community, the families, and the children in it. Relevance also suggests that the practitioners need to find meaning in what is happening too. They should think about their own interests and talents and those of colleagues, and try to think of ways to introduce or use them with children in appropriate ways. The courage to be spontaneous on occasion and deviate from the plans is evident.

It could be said that authenticity is more about how and why you do something with children than what you do. That is, almost any topic or experience can be a wonderful learning experience for children—it all depends on two things:

1. whether it comes out of something they have demonstrated interest in or something the adult has good reason to believe they would be interested in; and
2. how the experience or opportunity is offered to children; that is, is it offered in ways that make sense and capture their interest?

Authenticity is closely related to context and depends on the setting and the timing. What is an authentic opportunity or experience in one program may not be in another. For example, looking at the natural world of plants and animals in authentic ways would have a different focus with a group of 4-year-olds in an inner-city program than it would with children in a rural area. In addition, what is an authentic opportunity or experience at one point with a child or group of children may not be at another time. For example, focusing on the Olympics is likely to have much more relevance and meaning around the time that it is happening than at other times.

Relevance and authenticity remind us to mention again the importance of linking what happens inside the early childhood program to children's and families' lives outside, to the community, to parents' expectations. Our vision is of a program that is connected strongly to its community in a variety of ways that enhance the work life of the practitioners, as well as the experience of children and their families.

COLLABORATION

Our vision contains a lot of principles, but none of these principles is worth much unless they are translated every day into practice, into the reality of the experiences of families, children, and practitioners. The emphasis in this book is on what you do, not just what you think.

Our vision works ultimately when there is collaboration, working together for a common purpose, with a shared vision. Our vision, in other words, requires a shared vision. In the way we have constructed and written this book, we have seen an integrity or wholeness in many of the principles, in that they apply equally to children, practitioners, and families. We think the term *collaboration* best suits the perspective that should permeate the whole culture of the program.

So, what brings about genuine collaboration? Collaboration can only happen on a foundation of genuine respect for others simply because they are human beings; even those who disagree, are challenging, critical, or uncooperative.

In addition, we have identified three critically important additional components:

1. interactions and relationships;
2. honoring diversity; and
3. viewing children as partners.

Interactions and Relationships Have Priority

Firstly, collaboration requires giving priority to constructive interactions and relationships. This means that the roles and responsibilities of practitioners are clear, but there is at the same time flexibility and a willingness to pitch in and do whatever needs to be done. Collaboration does not imply that everyone is expected to do everything well. While skills and expertise are acknowledged and respected, no one's contribution is valued above another's.

For children, prioritizing relationships and interactions does not mean giving less priority to children's learning. In fact, the opposite is the case; encouraging relationships actually enhances and broadens children's learning. We would want an early childhood program to recognize that much valuable learning happens through relationships and interactions with others rather than in isolation. There is much evidence of collaboration, teamwork, collective problem solving, and compromise. Children are not forced to always spend time with other children but are supported to have a choice. They are also helped to acquire the skills and sensitivities needed to work effectively with others in ways that are satisfying and pleasurable. This means that learning how to engage others, to show care, to listen—in other words, to interact with and relate to others—is treated as being as important as more traditional kinds of learning.

Prioritizing relationships and interactions with families means viewing them not as an optional extra to add to the job of working with children but as an integral part of their work. It also acknowledges that genuine relationships when they work well are two-way; that is, our vision of parent–professional relationships is one where parents are active contributors to the relationship rather than passive recipients.

Diversity and Individuality Are Honored

There is openness to the views and perspectives of others, including colleagues, families, and children. Throughout the operation of the program, there is evidence that individual strengths, talents, and abilities are identified and people are encouraged to develop them to use on behalf of the group. Anyone's success is celebrated as everyone's success. Effective teams, as well as effective communities, emerge not when everybody is good at the same things, but when individuals make contributions that complement the contributions of others. At the same time, a great place to work with children, to be a child, and to have a child placed extends people and helps them grow and change, provides challenges, and supports reasonable risk taking. There is help to meet challenges and cope with difficulties, and someone to pick you up and offer encouragement when things don't work out.

In our view, programs that are good for children and families embrace diversity of all kinds. There is a feeling of acceptance and openness. There is a distinct absence of feelings of constraint or as though there is one right way to do things, to work with or rear children, or constrained notions of what it means to be a "good" or "clever" child. This does not mean that there is a feeling that "anything goes," but it does mean that difference is not automatically rejected or responded to with skepticism or fear, and there is a predisposition to look positively at it. Differences in culture, race, language and religion; differences in ability, gender, lifestyle, sexual orientation, and political views are accepted and respected. Furthermore, differences are seen not as problems but as sources of enrichment to the program, even when they generate discomfort.

We have embedded discussions of diversity throughout this book because that is the way we believe it should be in ECE programs. Diversity is not something you do, is not something you focus on at a particular time or through particular experiences and materials, but it is pervasive. Honoring diversity is not about "doing cultures"; rather, it's part of the culture of the program.

Honoring diversity is sometimes viewed skeptically by critics, who say that it promotes disunity. We believe that ECE programs should promote a strong sense of unity and community, working together for the same thing—children's well-being. We believe that accepting diversity, honoring it, and, at times, celebrating it actually leads to stronger bonds and connections. For us, it isn't a choice between unity or diversity; rather, it's unity *through* diversity.

We also encourage professionals to broaden their notions of types of diversity. Typically the word *diversity* makes us think first of race, culture, language, religion, social class, and sexual orientation. We may even use a different term to talk about people with diverse abilities. The more challenging kinds of diversity to live and work with are often those that do not have a label.

Children Are Viewed as Partners

We wrote at the beginning of this section that many of the principles in this book we see as applying equally to professionals, families, and children. However, we want to emphasize as we come to the end of this book what it means to act in ways that embrace the notion of children as collaborators and contributors. We do not see children as the objects or *recipients* of practice, but as partners in the process of planning and living in an early childhood program. Seeing children as collaborators or partners manifests itself as respect in action. It is a logical outcome of viewing children as strong, wise, and capable, no matter their age and abilities. There are no signs of children being viewed as "cute," or as objects of amusement. Babies and toddlers are treated with the same respect as older children. Discipline and limit setting are carried out with respect and care as well as firmness and, when this occurs, there is evident an orientation of being on the child's side rather than being antagonistic.

Seeing children, no matter how young they are, as contributors to their own learning and contributors to the life of everyone in the program necessarily requires focusing and building on children's strengths and interests rather than paying most attention to their deficits.

So there you have it—our vision of what early care and education can be. We don't expect everyone to have the same vision. We share ours with you in the hope that it will help you to create, alter, or affirm your own vision. Our final reminder is that, in the end, it's up to you and the people you work with, including your colleagues, families, and children. In the final analysis, diversity prevails as successful programs are about *action built on collaboration*. When done in authentic ways, no two look alike!

POSTSCRIPT

In Chapter 4 we wrote about two very different orientations that may be based on cultural background—individualistic and collectivistic. On the continuum of individualism and collectivism we find ourselves planted on the more individualistic end. Awareness of this does not mean that what we have written is free of either perspective, or that we present both perspectives in this book with equal prominence.

There are many places in the book where our individualistic perspective comes through. For example, we wrote about assertiveness as a desirable characteristic to nurture in children. We have written about the importance of self-valuing and esteem. The need to individualize routines for very young children, both in terms of timing and the ways things are done, has been emphasized. When we wrote about empowerment and empowering environments, we realized that everyone doesn't value a child-centered environment where the goal is independence, initiative, and engagement. It's hard for us to think of what empowerment and an empowering environment means to those with a strong collectivistic perspective and we would like to include that perspective. We invite readers with a more collectivistic orientation to create their own version of an empowering environment and share it with us!

We can be reached through the original publisher, Pademelon Press, at http://www.pademelonpress.com.au

References

Assagioli, R. (1972). *Act of will.* Baltimore, MD: Penguin.

Carr, M. (2001). *Assessment in early childhood settings: Learning stories.* London: Chapman.

Centre for Community Child Health. (2000). *Sharing a picture of children's development.* Melbourne: Australian Dairy Corporation.

Centre for Community Child Health. (2001a). *The cornerstone of quality in family child care and child care centers—Parent–professional partnerships.* Royal Children's Hospital Melbourne.

Centre for Community Child Health. (2001b). *The heart of partnership in family child care—Carer–parent communication.* Royal Children's Hospital Melbourne.

Dahlberg, G. (1999). *Beyond quality in early childhood education and care.* London: Falmer.

Derman-Sparks, L. (1989). *Antibias curriculum.* Washington, DC: National Association for the Education of Young Children.

Erikson, E. (1963). *Childhood and society.* New York: Norton.

Evans, R. I. (1973). *Jean Piaget, the man and his ideas.* New York: Dutton.

Gardner, H. (1983). *Frames of mind.* New York: Basic Books.

Gonzalez-Mena, J. (2002, September). Working with cultural differences: Individualism and collectivism. *The First Years: Nga TauTuatahi* [New Zealand Journal of Infant and Toddler Education], *3*(2).

Gonzalez-Mena, J. (2008). *Diversity in early care and education: Honoring differences.* New York: McGraw-Hill.

Gonzalez-Mena, J., & Eyer, D. (2007). *Infants, toddlers, and caregivers.* New York: McGraw-Hill.

Greenman, J., & Stonehouse, A. (1997). *Prime times—A handbook for excellence in infant and toddler programs.* Melbourne: Longman.

Lally, J. R. (1995, November). The impact of child care policies and practices on infant–toddler identity formation. *Young Children,* 58–67.

Maslow, A. H. (1970). *Motivation and personality.* New York: Harper and Row.

McVicker Hunt, J. (1961). *Intelligence and experience.* New York: Ronald Press.

NSW Department of Community Services, Office of Childcare. (2002). *NSW curriculum framework for children's services—The practice of relationships—Essential provisions or children's services.* Sydney: NSW Government Printer.

Piaget, J. (1926). *The language and thought of the child.* New York: Harcourt, Brace & World. (Original work published in 1923)

Piaget, J. (1930). *The child's conception of the world*. New York: Harcourt, Brace & World. (Original work published in 1926)

Piaget, J. (1952). *The origins of intelligence in children*. New York: International Universities Press. (Original work published in 1936)

Rogoff, B. (1990). *Apprenticeship in thinking*. New York: Oxford University Press.

Rogoff, B. (2003). *The cultural nature of human development*. New York: Oxford University Press.

Shareef, I. (1997). Personal conversation.

Shores, E., & Grace, C. (1998). *The portfolio book*. Beltsville, MD: Gryphon House.

Stonehouse, A. (1994). *How does it feel? Child care from a parent's perspective*. Canberra: Australian Early Childhood Association.

Stonehouse, A., & Gonzalez-Mena, J. (2001, November). Working with a high-maintenance parent: Building trust and respect through communication. *Child Care Information Exchange*, 57–60.

Thomas, A., & Chess, S. (1968). The origin of personality. *Scientific American, 223*, 102–109.

Vygotsky, L. (1978). *Mind in society: The development of higher mental processes*. Cambridge, MA: Harvard University Press.

Warren, R. (1977). *Caring*. Washington, DC: National Association for the Education of Young Children.

Werner, E. (1995, June). Resilience in development. *Current Directions in Psychological Science*, 81–85.

Index

Age and ability differences
  attachment and, 55
  body issues and, 58–59
  child development and, 66–67
  children with handicaps/special needs
    and, 119–120
  culture and, 63–64
  empowerment and, 69–70
  exploration and, 137
  fears and, 72–73
  group behavior and, 77
  home and, 82
  interactions and, 85, 86–87, 88–89
  judgment and, 89–90, 91
  in knowledge of child, 93–95
  learning styles and, 97–98
  major life events and, 100
  nature of, 52–53
  needs and, 101–104
  in outstanding qualities, 106–107
  play and, 109–111
  questions of children and, 112
  relationships and, 114
  temperament and, 124
  understandings and, 127–128
  voice and, 131
  will and, 134–135
  yearnings and, 140
  zones of proximal development and, 143
Aggression, 85–88, 90
Aims, as source of knowledge, 43–44
Anecdotal records, 156
Assagioli, R., 132
Assertiveness, 85–86
Assessment of children
  evaluation versus, 146
  learning how to learn and, 158–159
Attachment, 53–56
Authentic experiences
  culture of relevance and authenticity and,
    169–171
  in driving early care and education (ECE),
    3, 4–7

  nature of, 4–7
  projects in, 11–12
  themes versus, 10–11

Best guess, in planning process, 159–160
Body, 56–59
  bodily functions and, 57–58
  categories of information, 57
  physical activity needs and, 102–103

Carr, Margaret, 155
Centre for Community Child Care, 20, 22
Checklists, 158
Chess, Stella, 121–122
Child development, 64–67
  active support of, 36
  attachment in, 53–56
  bodily functions and, 57–59
  children with handicaps/special needs
    and, 117–118
  context in, 64–65
  developmental delays and, 36–37, 56,
    108–109
  empowerment in, 67–70
  exploration in, 136–138
  knowledge of child and, 93–95
  language in, 129–132
  and learning, 34–38
  limitations of developmental
    expectations, 38–39
  needs and, 101–105
  play and, 107–111
  seeing in a positive light, 12–13, 35–36
  zones of proximal development and,
    141–144
Children, knowledge about, 50–144
  attachment in, 53–56
  body in, 56–59
  culture in, 60–64
  development in, 64–67
  in driving early care and education (ECE),
    2–3
  empowerment in, 67–70

Children, knowledge about (*continued*)
  exploration in, 136–138
  fears in, 70–74
  group behavior in, 74–78
  home in, 78–83
  implications for practice, 53
  interaction in, 83–89
  judgment in, 89–93
  key aspects of, 51–53
  knowledge in, 93–96
  learning styles in, 96–98
  major life events in, 98–101
  needs in, 101–105
  outstanding qualities in, 105–107
  perspectives in, 147–148
  play in, 107–111
  questions in, 111–113
  relationships in, 113–116
  special issues in, 116–121
  temperament in, 121–125, 134–135
  understanding in, 125–128
  voice in, 129–132
  will in, 132–135
  yearnings in, 138–141
  zones of proximal development in,
    141–144
Children with handicaps/special needs
  additional support for, 116–121
  development and, 117–118
  play and, 108–109
Choices, in ECE programs, 10–12
Clarity, in parent–practitioner partnerships,
  23–25
Collaborative approach, 15–33, 171–174
  benefits of, 16
  children as partners in, 173–174
  communication in. *See* Communication
  conditions for parent–practitioner
    partnerships, 23–28
  diversity and, 16–19
  importance of, in ECE programs, 10, 146
  including families in, 161–162
  interaction priority in, 171–172
  nature of, 12, 19–21
  parent involvement versus, 21–22
  in planning for learning, 161
  relationship priority in, 171–172
Colleagues, as source of knowledge, 44–45
Commitment, in parent–practitioner
  partnerships, 28
Communication
  benefits for parents/caregivers, 28–29
  with children with special needs/
    disabilities, 121

  conditions for parent–practitioner
    partnerships, 23–28
  discussing difficult issues, 30
  importance of, 22–28
  information sharing in, 22
  natural flow of, 22–23
  nature of, 28–30
  strategies for, 31–33
  voice in, 129–132
Community
  expectations of, 45–46
  linking children and families with,
    46–47
  as source of knowledge, 45–47
Competence, in parent–practitioner
  partnerships, 26–27
Confidence
  of children, 13
  in parent–practitioner partnerships, 25
Connections, in parent–practitioner
  partnerships, 27–28
Continuity of care, 115
Creative thinking, in ECE programs, 9
Culture, 60–64, 165–171
  additive approach to, 61–62
  attitudes toward development and, 37
  body issues and, 58
  definition of "normal" and, 60, 65
  differences in attachment behavior and,
    54–55
  of environments that empower, 167–168
  individualism/collectivism continuum
    and, 80–82, 85, 86, 88, 174
  of joy, 167
  of linking care and education, 168–169
  questions of children and, 112–113
  of relevance and authenticity, 169–171
  sharing and, 84–85
  of thinking, 166
Current events, as source of knowledge,
  47–48
Curriculum, 1–14. *See also* Planning for
  learning
  defining, 3
  nature of, 1–2
  packaged, 48

Dahlberg, G., 116
Derman-Sparks, L., 64–65
Development. *See* Child development
Developmental delays, 36–37, 56, 108–109
Difficult child, 121–122
Disabilities. *See* Children with handicaps/
  special needs

Discipline and guidance
cultural issues in, 62
in ECE, 13–14
judgment and, 92–93
relationships and, 113–114
Diversity
among parents/caregivers, 19
categories in early childhood programs, 17–18
collaboration and, 16–19
in collaborative approach, 172–173
dangers of generalizations, 18
generalizations about parents/caretakers, 18–19
honoring, 17
kinds of, 17
in linking children and families with community, 46–47
nature of, 14
need for acceptance and, 17
in planning process, 161
Documentation, in information gathering, 153–154

Early care and education (ECE)
age range of children in, xi–xii, 4
authentic experiences and, 3, 4–7
collaborative approach in. See Collaborative approach
discipline and guidance in, 13–14
diversity and inclusion in. See Diversity
importance of, 2–3
key concepts in, 4
knowledge about the child in. See Children, knowledge about
linking care and education in, 168–169
nature of, vii
planning approach in. See Planning for learning
positive image of child in, 12–13, 35–36
program characteristics, 8–12
trends in, viii
Early childhood educators. See Practitioners
Easy child, 121–122
ECE programs. See Early care and education (ECE)
Empathy, in parent–practitioner partnerships, 26
Empowerment, 67–70
culture of environments that empower, 167–168
second language learning and, 130

Environment
culture of environments that empower, 167–168
as source of knowledge, 48, 148–150
Erikson, Erik, 102, 103–104
Evaluation
assessment versus, 146
of plans and programs, 162
Evans, R. I., 94
Exploration, 136–138

Failure to thrive, 56
Family. See also Collaborative approach
child in context of, 40–43, 64–67
including in planning process, 161–162
linking with community, 46–47
Fears, 70–74
Flexibility, of ECE programs, 9
Freud, Sigmund, 103–104
Friendship, among children, 115–116

Gardner, Howard, 105–106
Gender differences
attachment and, 55
body issues and, 58–59
child development and, 66–67
children with handicaps/special needs and, 119–120
culture and, 63
empowerment and, 69–70
exploration and, 137
fears and, 72–73
group behavior and, 77
home and, 82
interactions and, 85, 86–87, 88–89
judgment and, 91
in knowledge of child, 95
learning styles and, 97–98
major life events and, 100
nature of, 52
needs and, 103–104
in outstanding qualities, 106–107
play and, 109–111
questions of children and, 112
relationships and, 114
temperament and, 124
understandings and, 127–128
voice and, 131
will and, 134–135
yearnings and, 140
zones of proximal development and, 143
Geography, as source of knowledge, 48
Giftedness, 105–107
Grace, C., 154–155

Group behavior, 74–78

Habits of thought, judgment and, 90–91
Handicaps. *See* Children with handicaps/
   special needs
Hemingway, Ernest, 101
Home, 78–83

Incident reports, 157
Individuality
   in child development, 64
   in collaborative approach, 172–173
   individualism/collectivism continuum
      and, 80–82, 85, 86, 88, 174
Information gathering, 145–157. *See also*
   Knowledge sources
   assessment of children in, 146, 158–159
   daily informal conversations in, 146
   documentation in, 153–154
   environment and, 48, 148–150
   observing and recording behavior in,
      156–158
   organization of time and, 150–151
   portfolios in, 154–155
   routine daily living experiences and,
      151–152
Initiative, needs and, 104–105
Interactions, 83–89
   aggression, 85–88, 220
   in collaborative approach, 171–172
   problem solving and, 88–89
   sharing, 84–85
Interviews, in information gathering, 155
Investigations. *See* Projects

Journal writing, 157
Joy, culture of, 167
Judgment, 89–93

Knowledge of child, 93–96
Knowledge sources, 34–49. *See also*
   Information gathering
   aims and philosophy, 43–44
   child in context of family, 40–43, 64–67
   colleagues, 44–45
   community, 45–47
   current events, 47–48
   environmental context, 48, 148–150
   geographical context, 48
   professional knowledge, 34–40
   yourself, 48–49, 68–69, 113

Language, in child development, 129–132

Learning
   child development and, 34–38
   curriculum in. *See* Curriculum
   how to learn, 158–159
   motivation for, 13, 35, 113
   planning for. *See* Planning for learning
Learning communities, 44–45
Learning logs, 154–155
Learning stories, 155
Learning styles, 96–98
Limit-setting, 92–93

Major life events, 98–101
Maslow, Abraham, 103
McVicker Hunt, J., 10
Motivation
   intrinsic versus outside, 13
   for learning, 13, 35, 135
Multiple intelligences (Gardner), 105–106

Needs, 101–105
NSW Department of Community Services,
   12–13

Observing and recording behavior, 156–158
Outstanding qualities, 105–107

Packaged curriculum, 48
Parent involvement
   collaborative approach versus, 21–22
   kinds of, 21
Parents/caretakers
   benefits of communication for, 28–29
   child in context of family, 40–43, 64–67
   communication with practitioners. *See*
      Communication
   diversity among, 19
   generalizations about, 18–19
   relationships with children, 115
   working with, in ECE programs. *See*
      Collaborative approach
   yearnings for child, 139
Partnerships. *See* Collaborative approach
Passions
   projects and, 11–12
   yearnings and, 138–141
Philosophy, as source of knowledge, 43–44
Photographs, 158
Physical activity, need for, 102–103
Piaget, Jean, 93, 126, 128
Planning for learning, 159–162
   adult role in, 6
   approach to, 4

best guess in, 159–160
broad approach to, 7–12
collaboration in, 161
defined, 7
elements of planning, 160–161
focus on every child and all children in, 161
including families in, 161–162
information in. *See* Information gathering
ongoing evaluation in, 162
opportunities for learning in, 6–7
program characteristics, 8–12
systems and format for, 162–164
Play, 107–111
Portfolios, in information gathering, 154–155
Positive image of child, importance of, 12–13, 35–36
Power. *See* Empowerment
Practitioners
  boundaries of professional expertise, 19
  collaboration with parents and children. *See* Collaborative approach
  communication with parents/caregivers. *See* Communication
  information gathering by. *See* Information gathering
  working with parents/caregivers. *See* Collaborative approach
Problem solving, 88–89
Professional knowledge, 34–40
  boundaries of professional expertise, 19
  colleagues as source of, 44–45
  of development and learning, 34–38
  limitations of developmental expectations, 38–39
  other areas, 39–40
  sources of, 40
Programming. *See* Planning for learning
Projects
  nature of, 11
  place for, in ECE programs, 11–12

Quality Improvement and Accreditation System (QIAS), xii
Questions of children, 111–113

Relationships
  in collaborative approach, 171–172
  in knowledge of children, 113–116
Relevance, culture of, 169–171
Resiliency, 116–117

Rogoff, B., 37
Running records, 156–157

Safety, need for, 103
Second language learning, 129–132
Self-confidence
  of children, 13
  of practitioners, 25
Self-determination, 132–135
Self-esteem
  empowerment and, 68–69
  importance of, 174
Self-knowledge, 48–49, 68–69, 113
Self-regulation, 134
Shareef, Intisar, 69
Sharing, 84–85
Shores, E., 154–155
Slow-to-warm-up child, 121–122
Special needs. *See* Children with handicaps/special needs
Spontaneity, of ECE programs, 9
Stonehouse, Anne, 33

Taking turns, 135
Tape recordings, 158
Teachers. *See* Practitioners
Temperament, 121–125, 134–135
Themes, cautions for using, 10–11
Thinking, culture of, 166
Thomas, Alexander, 121–122
Time, organization of, 150–151
Time samples, 157
Transition times, 150–151, 152
Trust, need for, 102

Understandings, 125–128

Videos, 158
Violence, fears of children and, 71
Voice, 129–132
Vygotsky, Lev, 141–144

Warren, Rita, 40
Werner, E., 118
Will, 132–135

Yearnings, 138–141
Yourself, as source of knowledge, 48–49, 68–69, 113

Zones of proximal development (ZPD), 141–144

About the Authors

Janet Gonzalez-Mena has experience as a preschool teacher, home visitor, child care director, family child care coordinator, and supervisor of a pilot program of therapeutic child care for abused infants, toddlers, and preschoolers. She was on the faculty of the Child and Family Studies Program at Napa Valley College for 15 years. She has been on the faculty of the Program for Infant Toddler Care–Training of Trainers Institutes since 1991. Since 1999, she has been part of a training project called *Beginning Together,* which is designed to promote inclusion of children with disabilities into early care and education programs. She has written a number of textbooks and training manuals, including *Diversity in Early Care and Education, Caregiving Routines,* and *Bridging Cultures in Early Care and Education.* Janet has a M.A. in Human Development from Pacific Oaks College.

Anne Stonehouse is currently working as a consultant, editor, and author in the field of early childhood. Previously, she was an academic at Monash University (1996–2000) and the Northern Territory University (1985–1996). She has worked in Australia and overseas for over 35 years and has published widely. The second edition of *Prime Times: A Handbook of Excellence in Infant and Toddler Care* (co-authored with Jim Greenman) was published in 2007. She has undertaken several significant consultancies and writing projects in outside-school-hours care and family child care. She is the author of a curriculum framework for early childhood programs in New South Wales.

In recognition of her contribution to children and children's services, Anne was appointed a Member of the General Division of the Order of Australia in 1999.